A Foucault Primer

A Foucault Primer

Discourse, Power and the Subject

Alec McHoul and Wendy Grace

NEW YORK UNIVERSITY PRESS
Washington Square, New York

First published 1993 by Melbourne University Press
First published in the U.S.A. in 1997 by
NEW YORK UNIVERSITY PRESS
Washington Square
New York, N.Y. 10003
Reprinted 1998, 2000, 2002, 2003, 2007.

ISBN-13 978-0-8147-5480-1
ISBN-10 0-8147-5480-5

CIP data available from the Library of Congress

Contents

Preface

This book is intended as a brief introduction to the work of the philosopher and historian, Michel Foucault (1926–84). It is directed at undergraduates and others who are beginning to read his work and may be in need of a conceptual overview. The book comes out of a much larger project on Foucault's work. So what we present here is very much a cut-down version of our writing on the topic. It began when we were working as lecturer and student in a course on discourse analysis at Murdoch University, and continued via Wendy Grace's honours thesis (1992) on Foucault's feminist reception. It is very much a collaborative project between teacher and student, working in as collegial a way as that institutional arrangement can allow.

In this book we have very few axes to grind, and we have deliberately omitted—for reasons of available space—many of our misgivings about both Foucault's work and, more especially, other people's commentaries on it. Our aim here is exegetical rather than critical. This said, however, a few basic assumptions underlie our attempt to describe Foucault's work for beginners.

First, for complex reasons which we have no space to elaborate on here, we do not believe that Foucault provides a definitive theory of *anything* in the sense of a set of unambiguous answers to time-worn questions. In this respect, there is little benefit to be gained from asking what, for example, is Foucault's theory of power? Nevertheless, his work clearly involves various types of theoris*ation*. This is because we regard Foucault as first and foremost a philosopher who does philosophy as an interrogative *practice* rather than as a search for essentials. His investigations are conceptual, and the main concepts he approaches in his work—discourse, power and the subject (among others)—seem to us to be geared towards what he called an 'ontology of the present'. That is, Foucault is asking a very basic philosophical question: who are we? Or perhaps: who are we *today*?

Secondly, Foucault, like many continental European thinkers, does not separate philosophy from history in the way that many English-speaking philosophers do. The question of the ontology of the present (who are we today?) entails for him the question of the *emergence* of the modern human subject along a number of conceptual fronts. If, that is, we want to know who we are in terms of either the disciplines (or forms of knowledge) we have of ourselves, or the political forces which make us what we are, or our 'internal' relations to ourselves, we are necessarily faced (according to Foucault) with historical forms of enquiry. But at the same time Foucault is no historical determinist. Things, he insists throughout his work, could easily have been different. What we are now is not what we must *necessarily* be by virtue of any iron laws of history. History is as fragile as it seems, in retrospect, to be fixed. But, for Foucault, history is never simply in retrospect, never simply 'the past'. It is also the medium in which life today is conducted. In a brief phrase: Foucault is the philosopher and historian of 'otherwise'.

Thirdly, it is common nowadays to treat Foucault's work in terms of relatively fixed 'periods'. According to some commentators, his work divides into three phases: the first concentrates on the description of discourses or disciplines of knowledge (particularly the human sciences); the second turns to political questions of power, and the control of populations through disciplinary (for example, penal) practices; and the third involves some apparently new discovery of a 'theory of the self'. More alarmingly, some commentators have tied these radical shifts to changes in Foucault's personal biography (J. Miller, 1993). By contrast, we want to say both 'yes' and 'no' to this periodisation of Foucault's work. On the one hand there are clearly differences of focus and intensity as his work alters and develops. On the other, the general question of the ontology of the present remains. Not surprisingly, Foucault's own work is a matter of both continuity and discontinuity.

Foucault's early work (from *Madness and Civilisation* to *The Archaeology of Knowledge*) pays a great deal of attention to epistemic questions, or questions of knowledge. The 'units' of knowledge, at this time, are called 'discourses'. But political questions and questions about the subject are never far from the surface. Likewise, in the supposedly 'middle phase' of his work (marked mostly clearly by *Discipline and Punish* and the first volume of *The History of Sexuality*), Foucault is often presumed to have taken on the more overtly political questions of control, management, surveillance and policing, and shifted his attention from discourse and knowledge to the body and its politicisation. Yet *Discipline and Punish*, to take only one example, openly declares itself to be 'a correlative history of the modern soul and of a new power to judge' (1977a:23). It is easy to remember the power and the judgement but to forget the question of the subject ('the soul')—and indeed to forget the fact that the famous powers of judgement are exercised in, as, and through, disciplines or discourses. Then in the last works (especially the second and third volumes of *The History of Sexuality*), it is common enough to find that 'the subject' has suddenly burst on to the scene—at the expense, as it were, of the discursive and the political (McNay, 1992). Yet 'the subject' is in evidence throughout Foucault's work—albeit under different aspects, tensions and methods of analysis. This supposedly new 'ethical' questioning of the subject (in terms of the relations one has with oneself) is just as political a question, however, as that of 'external' surveillance or the coercion of the confessional. Perhaps it is true that in ancient Greece and Rome (the periods Foucault studies in these last volumes) there was less disciplinary (scientific) or political-legal control over human conduct. But it *was* controlled—perhaps, for some, almost entirely by oneself. And this, too, is a political question.

In this way, then, we find a similar question being asked—who are we now?—through a variety of different means and thematised concepts: discourse, power and the subject. Indeed, Foucault himself offered strikingly similar descriptions of the seminal works from each of his supposed periods. *The Archaeology of Knowledge*, he writes, is not about (the then fashionable) question of structure; rather, 'like those that preceded it . . . [it] belongs to that field in which the questions of the human being, consciousness, origin, and the subject emerge, intersect, mingle and separate off' (1972:16). Similarly, *Discipline and Punish* offers an analysis—albeit with a different focus—of a similar set of questions about who we are. It is 'a genealogy . . . of the modern "soul"' and, moreover:

> It would be wrong to say that the soul is an illusion, or an ideological effect. On the contrary, it exists, it has a reality, it is produced permanently around, on, within the body by the functioning of a power. (1977a:29)

Then, having detailed this 'theoretical shift' of focus from discursive practices to studies of power, in the introduction to the second volume of *The History of Sexuality* Foucault goes on to describe his second 'shift' as follows: 'It seemed appropriate to look for the forms and modalities of the relation to self by which the individual constitutes and recognizes himself *qua* subject' (1986a:6). In these shifts of concentrations from discourse to power and the subject, something is therefore retained: the broad philosophical question about who we are, constituted historically in terms of both what has been and its fragility.

In this book, therefore, we treat each of these concepts as a separate but related aspect of Foucault's ontology of the present. His approaches to these aspects of ourselves today can be framed as a set of questions:

- who are we in terms of our knowledges of ourselves?
- who are we in terms of the ways we are produced in political processes?
- who are we in terms of our relations with ourselves and the ethical forms we generate for governing these?

These amount to separate questions, respectively, about discourse, power and the subject. But their proximity to one another, and the historical fragility of each of them, cannot be ignored.

Our ways of approaching the concepts of discourse, power and subjection in Foucault are not identical in each case. In Chapter 1 we offer a general overview of Foucault's disciplinary area—the history of ideas—and his critical interventions into this field. The approach we take, however, is not a particularly 'Foucauldian' or 'genealogical' one at this stage. Rather it is, in itself, more like a traditional history of ideas. But, for this reason, we hope it is more accessible for the beginner. Chapter 2 consists, again, of a general discussion of Foucault's concept of discourse and puts particular stress on his own reflections on this concept rather than looking at how it works in actual analyses such as *Madness and Civilisation* or *The Birth of the Clinic*. In Chapter 3, we change direction somewhat. Although this chapter gives a general introduction to Foucault's ideas on power, and gives examples of his use of the concept, it also goes somewhat further than this and queries some of the secondary interpretive work in the area. The final chapter attempts to introduce Foucault's work on the subject and subjection via a detailed exegesis of the contents of his last works on sexuality. But in addition, at the end, it looks at how this work has been read by (particularly feminist) critics and suggests that there remain problems with their criticisms. To this extent, we end by arguing that Foucault's work has not yet been fully exploited for its possible contributions to contemporary debates on questions of gender and sexuality.

Acknowledgements

Several colleagues have helped our understanding of Foucault to develop into this book. In particular we would like to thank Toby Miller, Tom O'Regan, Bob Hodge, Teresa Ashforth, Jeff Malpas, Alison Lee, John Frow, Ian Hunter, Niall Lucy and Gary Wickham. Kind assistance with the editing and production of the book was provided by Susan Hayes, Garry Gillard, Nicola Rycroft, Venetia Nelson and Ken Ruthven—and we extend our thanks to them. We would especially like to thank Ken for his continuing encouragement of the project and, above all, for the sympathetic and meticulous work he has done on our drafts.

This book is dedicated to the memory of H272, Discourse Analysis, and to all who suffered it.

Murdoch University
May 1993

1

Foucault's Counter-history of Ideas

General background: discourse, power and knowledge

Of the three main Foucauldian concepts introduced in this book—discourse, power and the subject—the last is probably the most complex. As an orientation to Foucault's overall rethinking of his field—the history of ideas, or 'the history of systems of thought', as he preferred to call it—we will concentrate in this chapter only on the first two: discourse and power. But we must add to this a more direct consideration of the history of ideas itself and its own central concept, knowledge.

For the sake of exposition, we can say that Foucault's contribution to the history of ideas involves a rethinking of three central concepts: *discourse* (which had traditionally been the province of *structural linguistics*); *power* (particularly as it was analysed in *Marxist* philosophy in France); and *knowledge* (as the main focal point of *the history of ideas*). This multi-conceptual rethinking can be summarised by turning to Dreyfus and Rabinow's (1982) description of Foucault's overall project: to go 'beyond structuralism and hermeneutics', which were arguably the dominant methods of Foucault's own times.

Structuralism, for example in the work of the anthropologist Claude Lévi-Strauss, attempted to find the 'deep' or 'hidden' structures (taxonomies and hierarchies) at the very base of myths (such as the Oedipus myth). It tried to discover, by means of a *reductive* analysis, the objective and universal constituents of all human thought. In a structuralist analysis, there is no room for local or distinctive interpretations of a myth. The particular mythic text, collected 'in the field' by the anthropologist, is useful only as 'data' to confirm or disconfirm the supposedly underlying mythic *structure.*

Hermeneutics, by contrast, used a more interpretive method derived from phenomenology. Phenomenologists believe that the objective world described and analysed by structuralists is in fact a product of human consciousness and its interpretive processes. Therefore hermeneutics (named after Hermes, the messenger of the gods) allowed for differences of interpretations. In place of structuralism's objective structures, it turned instead to those acts of consciousness which produce local, and often highly specific, readings of texts.

Unlike the structuralists, Foucault does not hold that any essential or 'real' structure underpins particular 'events' or historical materials (such as myths and texts). The local and the particular, he argues, are always inserting their differences. But this insistence on the singularity of events is not the same as that which we find in hermeneutics. Foucault does not rush from structuralism to the phenomenological extreme and argue that 'reality' is constructed out of human consciousness and its ability to perform interpretations. In this way he avoids the seriously 'apolitical' defects of both traditions of thought. For Foucault, 'ideas' are neither mere effects of 'real' structures nor the 'baseline' from which reality is constructed.

Going 'beyond' structuralism and hermeneutics, Foucault rejects phenomenology outright. In the Foreword to the English edition of *The Order of Things* (1970:xiv), he suggests that whereas the genesis of structuralism is something his counter-history must at least account for (rather than rely on), at the same time, 'if there is one approach that I do reject . . . it is that (one might call it, broadly speaking, the phenomenological approach) which gives absolute priority to the observing subject'.

In traditional philosophical terms, Foucault steers away from—rather than between—the Scylla of (structuralist) realism and the Charybdis of (phenomenological) idealism.

How then does Foucault 'go outside' these forms of thinking, which could be said to have dominated his times? One way to answer this question is to look at the emergence of his rethinking of power, knowledge and discourse. And this means examining the central disciplines in which these three concepts were traditionally thought, namely Marxism, traditional history of ideas and structural linguistics, respectively. In the 1960s and 1970s, severe problems were emerging in all three of these critical discourses. Internal as well as external, these problems could be called, though the term is too dramatic, a 'crisis'. But if, by 'crisis', we mean a gradual and uneven splitting of the complex network of ideas formed by these critical disciplines, then the term will suffice. Foucault's work can then be read as an exploitation of the 'crisis', a moment in which to shift the very terrain of social and political critique itself. Rather than repair the breaks and tears opened up by the crisis (by providing continuity to the flows of Marxism, history of ideas and structuralism) Foucault sought new ways of thinking outside them.

For, by the mid-1960s, the very notion of continuous progress in both the human and the natural sciences, and between scientific 'stages', was itself in jeopardy. Furthermore, scientific change was no longer thought of as something brought about by a special creative subject or scientific 'hero' (an Einstein or a Freud, for example) who could be called upon to effect a theoretical revolution. The very notions of 'creative subject' and 'historical agent' were themselves 'in crisis'. Because they were part of the gap to be dealt with, they could not be enlisted as part of the solution.

Consequently, Foucault's counter-history of ideas had to be worked out so as to avoid giving primacy to the ideas of 'the individual' and of 'subjectivity'. Instead, Foucault thought of the human subject itself as an effect of, to some extent, subjection. 'Subjection' refers to particular, historically located, disciplinary processes and concepts which enable us to consider ourselves as individual subjects and which constrain us from thinking otherwise. These processes and concepts (or 'techniques') are what *allow* the subject to 'tell the truth about itself' (Foucault, 1990:38). Therefore they come before any views we might have about 'what we are'. In a phrase: changes of public ideas precede changes in private individuals, not vice versa.

In response to a further condition that the 'crisis' demanded, Foucault's counter-history also had to conceive of bodies of knowledge (discourses) as potentially *dis*continuous across history rather than necessarily progressive and cumulative. This is a major theme in Foucault's work generally, and has often led him to be called a (or even 'the') philosopher of discontinuity. Foucault's analysis of scientific change as discontinuous shows that it is not seamless and rational; that it does not progress from stage to stage, getting closer and closer to the truth; that it is not guided by any underlying principle which remains essential and fixed while all around it changes. This 'thesis' of discontinuity is indeed a key element in his analysis and critique of 'official' or 'dominant' knowledges. It also enters into his investigations of those forms of knowledge which are much less official, such as the knowledges which medical and psychiatric patients, criminals and sexual perverts, for example, have of themselves. But it is only one element among others. As we show in Chapter 2, Foucault's idea of 'discontinuity' is far from being just another essential principle behind all historical change.

The discourses of Marxism, history of ideas and structural linguistics (and, perhaps to a lesser extent, literary studies and psychoanalysis) were the main 'broken strands' in the network of ideas which faced Foucault in the mid to late 1960s. His first main theoretical texts—*The Order of Things* (1970) and *The Archaeology of Knowledge* (1972)—attempted to account for their emergence under the general rubric of 'the human sciences'. In what follows, we will take each strand separately, although parallels and congruences between all three disciplinary areas will be evident.

Marxism

By the late 1960s, the stock-in-trade concepts of mainstream Marxist political economy were increasingly seen as too mechanistic and deterministic to account for the plurality, diversity and fragmentation of late capitalism. Two such concepts were those of 'economic base' and 'ideological superstructure'. In classical Marxism, the 'real' economic conditions in a given period (especially the means of producing commodities and the question of which social classes own them) were known as the 'base'. This 'base' was believed to 'give off' the less tangible aspects of society: its laws, its beliefs, its ideology, its culture and so on. Hence a base–superstructure model is one in which material conditions (economic 'realities') determine ideas (types of consciousness).

This base–superstructure model and the economic determinism it implied were at risk in a number of respects. Science and technology had changed so much that the continued material existence of the world was itself in jeopardy. The Cuban missile crisis of 1962, for example, revealed the dependence of 'economic' factors on even more basic technological phenomena. Yet at the same time there was a growing awareness that nuclear technologies were themselves the product of scientific *ideas*. It began to look as if the domain of ideas (the superstructure) was not quite so irrelevant to an understanding of the most crucial foundations and uncertainties of twentieth-century life as earlier Marxists had thought.

Furthermore, the classical Marxist model seemed unable to cope with the new kinds of struggle emerging in so-called post-industrial societies. These struggles centred as much on race, gender and ecology as on purely economic considerations such as class (ownership or non-ownership of the means of production). The 'classical' class struggle of the nineteenth and earlier twentieth centuries became diversified, and not just because of an increasingly complex division of labour and a breakdown in strict class identifications. Class-based struggles were now related to 'other' struggles, such as those of blacks, women, environmental groups and gays.

In addition, the industrial 'base' of capitalism itself was beginning to shift away from its traditional sector, the 'heavy' industries, and towards ideas- or knowledge-based forms of production (such as computing, education, cinema, and information systems). The 'mode of production' was thus under threat from the 'mode of information' as the prevailing form of social existence (Poster, 1984). What was to count as industrial base (production) and what as superstructure (ideas, information) was now much less clear than it had been even a generation earlier (Smart, 1983; Williams, 1973). Moreover, Marxist analysts continued to argue that, despite such vast and sweeping changes, 'bourgeois domination' appeared to be surviving. There was no sign of that impending 'degeneracy' which had been predicted by the classical model. In fact, capitalism became arguably stronger and more entrenched as the critical discourses suffered their own various crises. Capital itself never really seemed to suffer from the so-called 'crisis of capitalism'. To this extent, it was now quite obvious that the forms of critical analysis which had suited nineteenth-century entrepreneurial capitalist formations had no place in either advanced industrial or post-industrial society. No less important to this political fragmentation were the failures of 'official' bureaucratic Marxism: the gulag, Hungary, Czechoslovakia, and so on.

Looking back from a vantage point of some fifteen years on the late 1960s (and particularly the student movements formed around the events of 1968), Foucault saw the situation like this:

> It is a case of movements which, very often, have endowed themselves with a strong reference to Marxism and which, at the same time, have insisted on a violent critique *vis-à-vis* the dogmatic Marxism of parties and institutions. Indeed, the range of interplay between a certain kind of non-Marxist thinking and these Marxist references was the space in which the student movements developed—movements that sometimes carried revolutionary Marxist discourse to the height of exaggeration, but which were often inspired at the same time by an anti-dogmatic violence that ran counter to this type of discourse. (1990:19)

The paradoxes of this situation ('exasperated dogmatism') are evident enough. A new type of critical analysis was needed which could account not only for new kinds of social fragmentation (different social types or 'subject positions') but also the absence of both a singular and unique basis of social existence (the production of material commodities) and a single central contradiction in society (class struggle). This form of critique would have to be sensitive to diverse, local and specific—even marginal or 'deviant'—practices and their effects. While critical social theory had to retain something equivalent to a theory of domination, it had to jettison Marxism's supposedly *necessary* connection between 'power' and economy. Even the much more flexible idea of determination in the 'last instance' (Althusser, 1970) had to be dropped as an explanatory necessity.

In addition, the necessary centrality of a particular class (classically, the proletariat) to the struggle against 'domination' had to be critically rethought. A class could no longer be seen to act as a 'subject in history'—and yet neither could it be a purely determined economic effect. To this extent the stress on class analysis itself had to be dropped or at least restricted or supplemented. It needed to be replaced by a theory of constraint (or 'structure') and enablement (or 'agency'), locked into a broader conception of society than economistic models had allowed. Such a theory would need to think of the 'wielders' of power as being just as inextricably caught in its webs as the supposedly powerless. It would have to see power in terms of *relations* built consistently into the flows and practices of everyday life, rather than as some *thing* imposed from the top down. In short, the predicament of Marxism showed the limitations of mechanistic determinism, and the need for a more subtly historical and detailed analysis of the local and specific effects of power. This, among other things, is what Foucault was to provide.

History of ideas

In the field known as 'history of ideas', the late 1960s and early 1970s saw a growing series of problems at least equal to those in Marxism. Indeed Marxism itself had been a main contributor to the history of ideas wherever a critical reading was required. Naturally enough, it had tended to argue that ideas were merely 'superstructural' effects of 'real' economic forces: as modes of production had progressed from feudalism through capitalism to socialism, so too had the various 'knowledges' which went with them. Marxism always appeared to provide a critical alternative to 'mainstream' approaches. What were these?

In France, the field called 'history of ideas' has always been very diverse, and has taken on a number of different titles: history of reason, history of science, history of knowledge(s), history of rationalities, and—with Foucault—history of systems of thought. But prior to Foucault, the two mainstream philosophies derived by and large from Hegel and Husserl respectively. The Hegelian tradition entered France in the 1930s via the ideas of Jean Wahl, Henri Lefebvre, Alexandre Koyré and especially Jean Hippolyte (Foucault's teacher and, later, colleague). Indeed, Hegelian philosophy was well established by the time Foucault came to study the subject in high school (Eribon, 1992:15–23). Its basic tenet was that a form of universal reason existed behind the 'surface' forms of human knowledge. Thus the 'progress of reason' could be discerned working its way through history as an immaterial but ever-present *Geist* or spirit. It was therefore profoundly *continuist*: each 'stage' of history was marked for its continuity in terms of the progress of universal reason, rather than for its distinctiveness and difference. Hegelianism was therefore a major theoretical influence on Marxist thinking at this time, since it provided the basis of dialectical thought: a general principle of historical change, which postulated that any form of thought would eventually transform, not into its negation, but into a synthesis of itself *with* its negation.

While Hegel's position is sometimes referred to as 'phenomenological' (largely because his *Phenomenology of Spirit* [1807] had most impact on French philosophy), it should not be easily confused with the phenomenological tradition which stems from the work of Husserl. The uptake of Husserl, in France, was largely the province of the philosopher Maurice Merleau-Ponty and of the existentialists, especially Jean-Paul Sartre. According to the existential interpretation of Husserl, the basic principle underlying historical change and transformation was not an abstract spirit but the irremediable freedom of individuals to create anew out of the 'raw material' from which they had been created. On this (idealist) interpretation, human thought or consciousness is supreme, and capable of transcending any apparently fixed, given or determining conditions. In analysing the history of thought, the phenomenological/existentialist school sought evidence of the human imagination triumphing over fixed traditions. Needless to say, existentialism tended to think of *itself* as being in this category. Yet existentialism also had an impact on Marxism, especially the so-called 'humanistic' or 'cultural' Marxisms of the 1970s. Sartre, for example, argued in the preface to his *Critique of Dialectical Reason* (1963, 1982) that fundamental existential freedom is compatible with a Marxist analysis of prevailing economic conditions.

However, the work of Gaston Bachelard, Georges Canguilhem and others was beginning to suggest—in different ways—that progressivist and continuist views of science—whether based in an abstract spirit or in fundamental liberty—were problematic. In particular, Canguilhem's (1968) meticulously detailed research on the history of biology showed that it could not easily be made subject to a universal theory of historical or 'ideological' change. With Canguilhem in mind, Foucault documents the shift away from continuism, saying that it 'was a question of isolating the form of rationality presented as dominant, and endowed with the status of the one-and-only reason, in order to show that it is only *one* possible form among others' (1990:27).

Since they are Foucault's main stalking-horses when it comes to theories of history, we should now unpack these notions of 'continuism' and 'progressivism'. After Canguilhem, it was no longer possible to hold unequivocally to the view that scientific theories change according to regular and universal patterns which, despite superficial changes, remain continuous through the history of science. Wherever Canguilhem had looked, it seemed that scientific changes were piecemeal, local and quite *ad hoc* affairs. They seemed to obey more a wild and Nietzschean than an orderly and Hegelian view of history. Eventually the very idea of there being a single rationale—a wider scheme of reference—for each and every scientific change, no matter how minute, could not be supported.

Along with continuism fell its close relative, the progressivist theory of scientific change: the view that a superior theory always replaces an inferior one, so that the 'same' science gets 'better and better' in moving closer and closer to the ultimate truth. Indeed, the new philosophies of science began to doubt the very grounds on which one theory could be called 'superior' to another simply because it came later in the day. The idea of *difference* between theories began to replace the idea of superiority versus inferiority.

Philosophers rejected the assumption that a new theory covers exactly the same terrain (but in a superior way) as the one it replaces. Instead, they came to think of theories as clusters of ideas which *produce* the very (physical, biological, economic) 'objects' which previously they had been thought merely to explain or describe. Again, this idea has its roots in Nietzschean thought, and is sometimes called 'constructivism'. If a theory, as the phrase has it, 'produces its own field', then it cannot be compared in any rational way with another rival theory. 'Nature' (or, say, 'madness') was no longer considered to exist 'out there'; the pure object could not be accessed independently of scientific ideas. Therefore neither 'nature' nor 'madness'—in some pure form—was available as a means of *comparing* different scientific theories about it.

To put it another way: if different theories are like so many yardsticks for measuring nature—and the more accurate the yardstick, the better the measurement—then (when it comes to *comparing* theories) it is obviously illogical to turn the relationship around and use 'nature itself' as the 'measure' of each theory's accuracy. It's simply not 'there' in a pre-measured form. But if not, what other measure is there? The way out of this vicious circle is to argue instead that our theoretical concepts actually 'provide for us what there really is (and isn't) in the universe' (Coulter, 1979:5). By adopting a constructivist position it was possible for historians of science to contemplate (and even condone) the existence of a *multiplicity* of contradictory and competing theories in a single disciplinary area, thus yielding multiple physicses, for example, or biologies or economic theories. It was no longer possible to say that the natural or exact sciences are unified while the social sciences are fragmented. Fragmentation had come to be thought of as the 'normal' state of scientific thinking in general.

Hence a new space opened up in which a history of ideas could stress discontinuity over continuity, multiplicity over progressivism, and difference over superiority/inferiority. It was no longer simply a case of tying changes in ideas to changes in an economic 'reality', or in the material 'needs' of society or, indeed, to 'empirical refutations' in the sciences themselves. In Marxism, linguistics and psychoanalysis, there was similarly a growing general dissatisfaction with the idea that human individuals or groups are directly responsible for either historical or epistemic changes. The view that such changes were the province of 'great thinkers' was coming under question, and it was surprising to discover how many previously respectable histories of ideas depended on this simplicism. Accordingly, histories of ideas which turned to the centrality of 'genius', 'creativity' and 'authorship' all began to suffer (Barthes, 1972, 1977). Instead, there was a general move to trace the paths of 'systems of thought' as objects in their own right, regardless of their thinkers. In the work of Foucault, these systems of thought came to be known as 'discursive formations' and the method of their analysis, at least in the first phase of his work, as 'archaeology'.

A typical object of investigation, which shows the critical difference between Foucault's archaeology and 'genius' theories, was what Foucault (1977b:113–38) called 'the author *function*'. This concept turns our attention towards the specific discursive and epistemic *conditions* which must be in place before we can even consider assigning the category of 'author' to an individual and, therefore, the property of 'authorship' to a text. These are the very conditions which make 'genius' and 'creativity' theories possible in the first place and, at the same time, the very thing which they overlook. What is more, texts have not always been assigned historically to the function of 'author': other categories have been used as the primary way of attaching meaning to texts. Finding the text's meaning in its author's 'mind' or 'intentions' is a historically contingent operation: for a long time it was not practised at all; it came to prominence briefly and is now starting to disappear (Williamson, 1989). But why do this? Why disturb such 'trusted' and commonsensical ways of operating? Foucault argues that:

> It is fruitful in a certain way to describe that-which-is by making it appear as something that might not be, or that might not be as it is. Which is why this designation or description of the real never has a prescriptive value of the kind, 'because this is, that will be.' It is also why, in my opinion, recourse to history—one of the great facts in French philosophical thought for at least twenty years—is meaningful to the extent that history serves to show how that-which-is has not always been; i.e., that the things

> which seem most evident to us are always formed in the confluence of encounters and chances, during the course of a precarious and fragile history . . . It means that they reside on a base of human practice and human history; and that since these things have been made, they can be unmade, as long as we know how it was that they were made. (1990:37)

Structural linguistics

In structural linguistics, what we have been calling 'the crisis' was somewhat different; it was, perhaps arguably, a matter of exhaustion. Structuralism, it is true, had generated much excitement for theorists in the 1950s and 1960s. Moreover, according to many accounts, the early Foucault shared much of its general epistemological equipment and methodology and was particularly influenced by the work of the structuralist Georges Dumézil (Foucault, 1971:27–8). But to take just one form of structuralism, semiotics (the analysis of signs of all sorts, linguistic and non-linguistic) had, by the early 1970s, emerged as a much wider form of cultural analysis than its parent, the structural linguistics of Ferdinand de Saussure. But still there had been no fundamental *theoretical* changes for the best part of half a century in the semiological/structuralist camp (Hawkes, 1977; Culler, 1975). French structural linguistics had been all but unaffected by the transformational-generative revolution effected in Anglo-American circles by Noam Chomsky. (And, in any case, there was every reason to think of Chomsky as ultimately continuous with the continental structuralist tradition exemplified by Lévi-Strauss (Lane, 1970)).

Roland Barthes' *Elements of Semiology* (1967, Fr 1964), for example, did little more than widen the scope of Ferdinand de Saussure's *Course in General Linguistics* (1974, Fr 1916), for example, by applying Saussurean concepts to such cultural objects as restaurant menus. To this extent, the problem was not so much one of 'crisis' as of repetition or sheer 'sameness', at least at the theoretical level. But significantly enough, it was Barthes' later (1978, 1981)—arguably post-semiotic—texts which helped lead the way out of this impasse, and towards the new emphasis on language and discourse in the human sciences known as the 'linguistic turn'.

This rethinking was political in its fundamental inspiration. First, Saussure's basic conception of the linguistic sign, as split into two aspects, the signifi*er* and the signifi*ed*, came in for criticism. The signified was, for Saussure, a *mental* representation or concept corresponding to any spoken utterance or written mark. The signifier was 'not the material sound, a purely physical thing, but the psychological imprint of the sound, the impression it makes on our senses' (Gadet, 1989:28). This notion of the signified, being the mental backbone (or meaning) behind the surface signifier (or sound-image), placed too much value on a naive theory of mind. In this sense, Saussurian structuralism came to be thought of in relation to bourgeois idealism: language had been reduced to ideas, concepts and psychological 'imprints'. On the other hand, replacing the notion of the signified with, say, a 'real' object as opposed to a purely psychological one—as was popular in positivist accounts of meaning—pointed in the direction of an equally pernicious realism and, thereby, again supposedly towards bourgeois thought (Coward and Ellis, 1977). Foucault documents his own objections to these views of language in the preface to *The Birth of the Clinic* (1973).

More generally, this impasse in structuralism led many thinkers to consider language and discourse as being something other than a representation of non-discursive 'reality', whether in the mind or in the real world. In essence, theories of the relations between language and the 'real' were abandoned in favour of theories relating linguistic element to linguistic element (Silverman and Torode, 1980). Semiotics and structuralism, that is, moved towards the signifier side of things. Discourse, then, took on the guise of a relatively autonomous, yet quite material, sphere in its own right. This position became known as the theory of the 'materiality of the signifier'. Hence there was a new semiology of the signifier, of discourse and of discursive relations which dropped its purely analytic stance and took on aspects of a political and historical critique, albeit of a vaguely Marxish kind. Language ceased to be the province of formal linguistics alone. It was reconceived as a social and political entity, the means by which what we know of the world can be created (rather than simply represented). The very term 'language' appeared insufficient to this task since it had always implied merely a *system* of representation—a kind of mechanism. The new term 'discourse' came increasingly to replace it. Yet 'discourse analysis' still meant something like 'the politics of communication' and was therefore a good distance from Foucault.

To this extent, it was necessary for the history of the *study* of language itself to be rethought. It was now necessary to show how these assumptions about language's relation to the world actually came about. What disciplines, forms of knowledge, or *discourses* (in Foucault's sense) had enabled this way of thinking? Starting with *The Order of Things* (1970)—in French *Les mots et les choses*, 'words and things'—Foucault began to undertake this very task: an archaeology of the human sciences, no less, and the history of their relations to thinking about language. In a field occupied, albeit precariously, by linguistic analysis, systems and taxonomies (based further on an underlying faith in the undisputed representational capacities of language), Foucault began to document the history of how this very field became possible. How did we get the idea that language represents something; that language is a *system and structure* of representation? How did this come to be accepted as 'what language really is'? In asking these critical questions, Foucault did not simply 'document' the historical emergence of the linguistic terrain. The conception of discourse mobilised in his historical studies eventually shifted that terrain rather than rebuilding on the old foundations.

Critique

This first phase in Foucault's work—where he worked out his *archaeological* approach to the history of knowledges—is essential to an understanding of what comes later, namely, Foucault's 'positive' and 'interventional' social and political writing. Indeed we will return to it in further chapters. But let us now go on to the second phase and, having roughly sketched the theoretical background, see how the reconfigured triplet of discourse, power and knowledge came, along with related concepts, to take its part in this 'positive thesis'. So now we must ask ourselves how, in the work of the 'middle period' (1977a, 1978a, 1979a, 1980a, 1980b), Foucault's analyses became 'critical', how they began to mesh with social and political problems and questions outside the rather confined space of academic specialism.

It is true that, from *Madness and Civilisation* to *The Order of Things*, Foucault had been concerned with how disciplinary knowledges functioned. But this had been part of an overall interest in coming to grips with the historical and philosophical problem of how bodies of ideas change and transform. And by and large the focus of attention was on the disciplines themselves, almost, but not quite, for their own sake. Hirst and Woolley (1982:164–96), for example, explain that *Madness and Civilisation* is *not* a history of psychiatry but rather an investigation of the conditions that made possible the eventual development of such a discipline. During the Renaissance, madness was not considered to be a disease or illness and the mad were not excluded from the rest of society. Rather they were considered to be under the influence of 'folly'—a benign, or even wise and revelatory, mode of thought. The great confinement of the mad was, therefore, neither a necessary nor inevitable development. Then, during the mid to late 1970s, Foucault began to focus his attention on questions of crime and sexuality: fresh topics which demanded a relatively fresh orientation, a critical operation of the concepts of power, knowledge and discourse. Accordingly, *Discipline and Punish* is not simply about the disciplines of criminology and its forebears; it is also about the subjects produced by techniques of punishment and confinement—criminals. Likewise, the first volume of the *History of Sexuality* is not simply about the various sexological disciplines; it is also about the sexual beings (the 'types') they brought into existence. Furthermore, at this time, Foucault began to consider questions of transgression and resistance in the face of the 'technologies' of punishment and sexual classification.

One element of this critical phase, therefore, involves an attention to subjugated or 'marginal' knowledges, especially those which have been disqualified, taken less than seriously or deemed inadequate by official histories. These might be called 'naive' knowledges, because they 'are located low down' on most official hierarchies of ideas (Foucault, 1980a:82). Certainly they are ranked 'beneath' science. They are the discourses of the madman, the patient, the delinquent, the pervert and other persons who, in their respective times, held knowledges about *themselves* which diverged from the established categories. One commentator refers to these people as 'unruly', as opposed to 'well-tempered', subjects (T. Miller, 1993). The knowledges (or forms of discourse) of these 'unruly' subjects might be particular, local and regional, or they might have wider, even international, currency. In at least two of his case studies, Foucault (1978a, 1980b) makes it clear that simply to 'repeat' these unruly positions, without commentary, may be a critical activity in itself, an act of resistance to the usual treatment of them by the various sciences. It is therefore problematic to interpret Foucault's archaeological method as one which simply 'unburies' the hidden or repressed discourses 'proper' to subjugated persons. In 'Politics and the Study of Discourse' (1978b), Foucault makes it clear that he has no interest whatsoever in revealing the previously hidden secrets of history. And when asked, 'Does your project include any effort to rehabilitate this other?' (for example, the silence of the mad person), Foucault answers very equivocally (1990:29). On the other hand, he *is* on record as supporting a resuscitation of subjugated knowledges:

> By subjugated knowledges I mean two things: on the one hand, I am referring to the historical contents that have been buried and disguised in a functionalist coherence or formal systematisation . . . Subjugated knowledges are thus those blocs of historical knowledge which were present but disguised . . . and which criticism—which obviously draws on scholarship—has been able to reveal. On the other hand, I believe that by subjugated knowledges one should understand something else . . . a whole set of knowledges that have been disqualified as inadequate to their task or insufficiently elaborated: naive knowledges, located low down on the hierarchy, beneath the required level of cognition or scientificity . . . It is through the reappearance of this knowledge, of these local popular knowledges, these disqualified knowledges, that criticism performs its work. (1980a:81–2)

Yet this way of working (repeating *or* revealing) also shows how official knowledges (particularly the social sciences) work as instruments of 'normalisation', continually attempting to manoeuvre populations into 'correct' and 'functional' forms of thinking and acting. Therefore Foucault also has an interest in examining the methods, practices and techniques by which official discourses go about this process of normalisation and, in the process, occlude forms of knowledge which are different from them, by dividing the normal person from the pathological specimen, the good citizen from the delinquent, and so on. One way in which this happens is when science transforms non-scientific discourses into 'data'—mere objects for analysis—and so produces an implicit (or even quite explicit) *hierarchy* of knowledges. So, for example, medicine makes 'diagnoses', by using 'symptoms' available from the 'data'. And the data, in this case, comprise the bodies of patients along with those (inferior) forms of knowledge which patients have about their bodies.

What is to count as 'truth'—for example, the truth about a person's sexuality or health—is therefore always the effect of specific kinds of techniques—the very kinds of institutional and discursive practices which Foucault analyses in *Madness and Civilisation* and *The Birth of the Clinic.* But, by way of contrast with these earlier studies, Foucault begins to ask questions of the *value* of these techniques. For example, in his case study of a nineteenth-century hermaphrodite, Herculine Barbin, Foucault (1980b:vii) begins by asking: 'Do we *truly* need a *true* sex?'. The question is far from being 'purely academic', as the phrase has it. He goes on to investigate how the medical and psychiatric sciences (among other discourses) have been preoccupied with assigning a single sex to all persons, and the consequent difficulties they have faced with cases of hermaphroditism. But now his point is not simply 'archaeological' in any arcane sense. He is writing as much about our current prejudices and schemes of thought *vis-à-vis* essential and unitary sexual identities as he is about the medical, legal, religious and psychiatric practices of the nineteenth century:

> The idea that one must indeed finally have a true sex is far from being completely dispelled. Whatever the opinion of biologists

> on this point, the idea that there exist complex, obscure, and essential relationships between sex and truth is to be found . . . not only in psychiatry, psychoanalysis, and psychology, but also in current opinion. We are certainly more tolerant in regard to practices that break the law. But we continue to think that some of these are insulting to 'the truth': we may be prepared to admit that a 'passive' man, a 'virile' woman, people of the same sex who love one another, do not seriously impair the established order; but we are ready enough to believe that there is something like an 'error' involved in what they do. An 'error' as understood in the most traditionally philosophical sense: a manner of acting that is not adequate to reality. Sexual irregularity is seen as belonging more or less to the realm of chimeras. That is why we rid ourselves easily enough of the idea that these are crimes, but less easily of the suspicion that they are fictions which, whether involuntary or self-indulgent, are useless, and which it would be better to dispel. Wake up, young people, from your illusory pleasures; strip off your disguises and recall that every one of you has a sex, a true sex. (1980b:x)

Few passages outside Foucault's interviews, public speeches and newspaper articles are more clearly polemical, and more clearly directed towards transgressions of what (it seems) has always counted, and must always count, as 'the truth'. Few are concerned more with the present day. Yet in the major works of this period, especially *Discipline and Punish*, Foucault is hardly polemical, rarely mentions transgression and confines himself to descriptions of the past. His style of presentation hardly ever appears 'negative'. He rarely makes an explicit statement about these practices being 'bad'. This has led some pro-Foucauldian scholars into assuming that Foucault's analytic descriptions should be mobilised *on behalf of*, for example, official governmental agencies (Bennett, 1992; Foucault, 1979b). Others, concerned to ensure that the uptake of Foucault's ideas should not entail adherence to a 'school' or 'manifesto', perceive the 'Foucault effect' as designating only a particular perspective in studies of the history of the present (Burchell et al., 1991). But this by no means excludes the possibility that Foucault's close historical descriptions can be used as assembled reminders and resources for critical action and interventional practice (O'Regan, 1992).

Foucault, then, is more than dubious about notions of absolute truth, or indeed of definitive philosophical answers to political questions. And he is far from believing that it is the task of intellectuals to provide such things. But this does not mean that 'there is no truth'. On the contrary, there can sometimes be many, each with its own rationality. But the question is: which of these, at any given period, comes to predominate and how? So instead of mobilising philosophy as the search for truth as such, Foucault tries to take this continual *desire* for a single truth (particularly on the part of the human sciences) as a topic of critical analysis and description. Then, as O'Regan says (1992:415), it is up to political activists to use these critical descriptions in their own ways and for their own purposes. This may seem a dereliction of political duty. But it has at least one virtue: it does not try to speak for others or to tell them what to do. 'When the prisoners began to speak', writes Foucault,

> they possessed an individual theory of prisons, the penal system, and justice. It is this form of discourse which ultimately matters, a discourse against power, the counter-discourse of prisoners and those we call delinquents—and not a theory *about* delinquency. (Foucault, 1977b:209)

It is therefore possible to contribute to political action not only by entering the fray but also by providing studies of official techniques of regulation, punishment, normalisation and so on to those groups which have a direct interest in their subversion. Consequently, in *I, Pierre Rivière* (1978a), Foucault and his co-workers do little more than reproduce many of the original nineteenth-century documents pertaining to the case. Rivière is an interesting and instructive case when it comes to understanding how the modern criminal is produced. He was a multiple murderer, but one with whom the authorities had a problem. He was caught up in a number of 'indecisions' between two official discourses on punishment, roughly those of the eighteenth and nineteenth centuries. The first involved forms of obvious and ritualistic public punishment of individual *bodies*. The second inaugurated control of *populations* by putting them under constant watch, under the gaze of scientific surveillance.

Rivière came to trial at a time when the old order of punishment by spectacular retribution had not yet met its demise and the new order was still in its infancy. The courts could not easily decide whether to 'make an example' of him (after the manner of the moral techniques of the eighteenth century) or whether to be 'humane' and condemn him to a life of continual observation. There was an effective dilemma, at the time, over what was to *count* as the official and proper discourse on the treatment of murderers. The emergent scientific discourses of medicine and proto-psychiatry had the same problems. For example, they wanted to know whether 'monomania'—a 'disease' in which sufferers become mad for a short period and then completely recover their rationality—actually existed. And if it did exist, to what extent could its existence 'excuse' a multiple murderer by making a culprit of the 'disease' rather than the individual?

In so far as Pierre Rivière is caught between these two moments of official dispute on the proper course of punishment, his own account—the lengthy 'confessional' narrative which he composed in prison—is continually kept at arm's length. The official 'sciences' (law, psychiatry, medicine) simply do not know how to *treat*, in both senses, Rivière's memoir. While scientific discourse may 'explain' crime, what the criminal himself knows becomes (for, say, criminology) part of the criminal conduct to be explained. It becomes, for example, a confession. Foucault's methodological problem is this: how *not* to join in these acts of official treatment? One strategy would be to offer a direct counter-analysis. But there are problems with simply inverting disciplinary procedures.

In his debate with a Maoist group, for example, Foucault argues that the strategy of setting up a court to try the police for their crimes constitutes merely a *repetition* of bourgeois forms of justice. Yet 'this justice must . . . be the target of the ideological struggle of the proletariat, and of the non-proletarianised people: thus the forms of this justice must be treated with the very greatest suspicion by the new revolutionary state apparatus' (1980a:27). The point is that a *technique*, whatever its 'content' or the polarity of its content, can be a technique of power in its own right. Critique can sometimes, therefore, consist in *ceasing* to do something; in ceasing to repeat the official technique.

For Foucault, no scientific discourse—whatever its claims—can represent the truth of crime, madness, sexuality and so on. It can only *treat* them, contain them somehow, within the 'sovereign' discourses of science. This is the power of one discourse in relation to another and, for Foucault, power is always a discursive *relation* rather than something which a person or group wields or bears. In order to try to avoid repeating such a relation (though the risk is ever-present) Foucault's technique involves what might be called a kind of lamination: building up citation upon citation, juxtaposing official and marginal discourses, quoting at length, rarely making heavily marked interpretive comments, allowing bits of cited text to carry the work, arranging and collecting historical fragments so that the order and arrangement of them, the technique of their montage perhaps, speaks for itself.

Foucault's critique of power, moreover, locates power at its extremities, where official discourses over-assert their authority (whether monarchical or democratic). These occur in the lawcourt or in the confessional, but always at the site of local, regional and quite material institutions such as those of torture or imprisonment. Here power always appears less legitimate, less legal in character. It seems that way in and of itself, regardless of any further commentary.

Another aspect of Foucault's critical method is that it locates power outside conscious or intentional decision. He does not ask: who is in power? He asks how power installs *itself* and produces real material effects; where one such effect might be a particular kind of subject who will in turn act as a channel for the flow of power itself. Foucault does not turn to the 'authors' of power but to the field of power:

> Let us not . . . ask why certain people want to dominate, what they seek, what is their overall strategy. Let us ask, instead, how things work at the level of those continuous and uninterrupted processes which subject our bodies, govern our gestures, dictate our behaviours etc. In other words, rather than ask ourselves how [for example] the sovereign appears to us in his lofty

> isolation, we should try to discover how it is that subjects are gradually, progressively, really and materially constituted through a multiplicity of organisms, forces, energies, materials, desires, thoughts, etc. We should try to grasp subjection in its material instance as a constitution of subjects. (1980a:97)

Power is not to be read, therefore, in terms of one individual's domination over another or others; or even as that of one class over another or others; for the subject which power has *constituted* becomes part of the mechanisms of power. It becomes the vehicle of that power which, in turn, has constituted it *as* that type of vehicle. Power is both reflexive, then, and impersonal. It acts in a relatively autonomous way and produces subjects just as much as, or even more than, subjects reproduce it. The point is not to ignore the subject or to deny its existence (as is the case with some forms of structuralism) but rather to examine *subjection*, the processes of the construction of subjects in and as a collection of techniques or flows of power which run through the whole of a particular social body.

We can therefore refer to a *terrain* of power which, for Foucault, is not to be taken as merely 'ideological' in the weak sense, where that term refers to any aspect of individual or collective consciousness. The effects of power, rather, are quite material, and potentially empowering; and their site is more often than not the body. Thus power is comprised of instruments for the formation and recording of knowledge (registers and archives), methods of observation, techniques of registration, procedures for investigation, apparatuses of control and so forth (Hacking, 1981, 1982). Foucault's critical method, then, tries to ensure that his 'discourse analysis' (which is more often than not highly descriptive) does not become merely another arm of official disciplinary sciences. It attempts to refrain from appropriating those discourses traditionally located 'beneath' science.

Foucault is the first major writer to pose the question of power in relation to discourse. Prior to Foucault, structural linguistics analysed the object of the 'text' via the methods of semiology and structuralism, while the psycho-social sciences turned by and large to the creative subjectivities of responsive readers. Foucault sought to place discourse(s) outside the opposition between the hard place of the objective text and the soft pulp of readerly subjectivity. For him, it neither resides in the givenness of the text, nor in the infinite interpretive possibilities open to a free-ranging reader. Instead it consists of determinate discursive practices which may equally well be on the side of writing as of reading. For it is essentially these practices which not only produce texts but also constitute the conditions of possibility for reading. Foucault's concept of discursive practice—and this may be the one intellectual debt he owes to structuralism—effectively eliminates the distinction between the 'subject' and 'object' of discourse. Since Foucault, discourse can no longer be relegated to the sphere of ideology; and yet neither can it have the certitude that Marxism would give to the economy and other 'real' orders.

Foucault removes the innocence of the discursive in its guise as either noble savage (pure text) or civilised child (pure human creativity). Discourse moves in, and as, the flows of power. Discourses—for example scientific discourses—never move outside the limits of power so as to be able to 'purely analyse' it. The structuralists' notion that 'ordinary' language always needs to be supplemented by an analysis of its 'truer' and 'deeper' meaning is effectively annulled. It is no longer possible to see discourses as 'surface' phenomena underpinned by a more 'real', but hidden, structure. Discourse can no longer be seen to be harmless, to have a mythically 'original' state. The 'origin' is a discursive myth—with its own history—and not a 'real presence' inhabiting an object or text (Derrida, 1976). Interpretation is nothing more than one discourse—usually a scientific one—trying to secure another within its bounds. Complete interpretation, then, is impossible. But while it may fail ultimately, it can nevertheless bring off the appearance of having quite adequately captured its 'object' by a series of techniques which 'stitch up' the imperfections in its representation of the 'other'. For Foucault it is essential to uncover these techniques, which are quite often material and can take effect at the level of the body.

Two such techniques are the confessional and the prison design known as 'the Panopticon', which we deal with in more detail in Chapter 3. It suffices for now to mention that these are techniques (in fact, sets of techniques) which attempt to *know* particular

2

Discourse

To look at how Foucault used the concept of discourse, we turn to those conceptual and methodological reflections on the historical 'discourse analyses' he had performed in his earlier works (1967, 1973), and especially the analyses in *The Order of Things* (1970). These reflections are to be found in *The Archaeology of Knowledge* (1972) particularly, but also in other texts of self-commentary (1971, 1978b).

Foucault thinks of discourse (or discourses) in terms of bodies of knowledge. His use of the concept moves it away from something to do with language (in the sense of a linguistic system or grammar) and closer towards the concept of discipline. We use the word 'discipline' here in two senses: as referring to *scholarly* disciplines such as science, medicine, psychiatry, sociology and so on; and as referring to disciplinary *institutions* of social control such as the prison, the school, the hospital, the confessional and so on. Fundamentally, then, Foucault's idea of discourse shows the historically specific relations between disciplines (defined as bodies of knowledge) and disciplinary practices (forms of social control and social possibility).

This is very different from other (especially Anglo-American) conceptions of discourse. In order to clarify what discourse is for Foucault, we need to address the following three questions:

- how has the term 'discourse' been used in the traditional (usually linguistic) disciplines?

- what was the basis, in Foucault's earlier work (1970, 1972), for his complete reconceptualisation of the idea of discourse?
- what are some of the political possibilities opened up by this rethinking of the concept?

Non-Foucauldian conceptions of discourse

Foucault's approach to discourse can be called a 'critical' approach, since it is geared towards a counter-reading of historical and social conditions and offers possibilities for social critique and renewal. This can rarely be said of the non-critical approaches stemming from linguistics, socio-linguistics and sociology (among other traditional disciplines). For the sake of exposition, let us separate these non-Foucauldian approaches into two groups: the *formal* and the *empirical* approach. English-speaking readers are more likely to be familiar with these two groups of approaches, perhaps, than continental ideas about discourse-as-knowledge; yet it will be worthwhile clarifying how these forms of discourse analysis operate. (For fuller discussions, see Hodge (1984) and McHoul (1993).)

The formal approach to discourse analysis considers discourse in terms of *text.* Its main precursors are the linguists Harris (1952) and Mitchell (1957). Following Harris, formalist discourse analysts work with variations of formal linguistic methods of analysis. Following Mitchell, they are interested in the social functions of language and often use (so-called) 'naturally occurring' samples of linguistic usage as data. Formalist discourse analysis is therefore very close to the disciplines known as socio-linguistics (Giglioli, 1982) and the ethnography of communication (Bauman and Sherzer, 1974; Gumperz and Hymes, 1972). Again, at other times, the formal approach is not called 'discourse analysis' but instead 'text linguistics' (or 'text grammars'). This variation, rooted in the Russian Formalist school (Lemon and Reis, 1965), connects it to those various forms of French structuralism (Saussure, Lévi-Strauss and the early Barthes) to which Foucault's (post-structuralist) treatment of discourse runs counter.

Despite this history, there is a sense in which formal discourse analysis can be critical. For example, the systemic functionalist school of linguistics, associated with Halliday (1973)—whose theoretical roots are also located in Russian formalism—has recently been rethought by such analysts as Hodge and Kress (1988) to generate a new approach called 'social semiotics' or 'critical linguistics'. This type of discourse analysis does not always relate to French critical discourse theory (such as Foucault's). Yet it offers a version of formal linguistics (Hallidayan systemic functionalism) which reads 'naturally occurring' texts as socially classed, gendered and historically located. More importantly, Halliday has been used (and re-thought) in relation to feminist theory and practice by, for example, Threadgold (1988). Threadgold's critical feminist linguistics has challenged simplistic arguments against, for example, the gendering of pronouns (Spender, 1980). Instead it has argued that discourse analysis should not examine how language *in general* is gendered but how gender-differential forms of *access* to particular registers and genres (ways of using language) have become normal and dominant through complex historical processes. So we should hesitate before we reject all formalist versions of discourse analysis out of hand. In their own ways, they offer genuine possibilities for critical intervention, though at a quite different level from Foucault's analyses (Fairclough, 1989).

But the possible critical and political uses of formal linguistic methods are only one side of the coin. At another extreme, the formalist approach is mechanistic. That is, it attempts to find general underlying rules of linguistic or communicative function 'behind', as it were, imagined or invented texts. In this way, the idea of discourse in this discipline becomes quite narrow and very different from Foucault's. It is much less of a diversified social and epistemological phenomenon and more of a formal linguistic system in its own right. For this reason, it seems to require a relatively narrow linguistic description. One extreme version of formalism, known as 'speech act theory', assumes that 'behind' forms of words which perform particular functions (speech acts) there exists a more general layer of pragmatic competence which has rules or conditions. The job of the speech act theorist is to discover these. Hence *paroles* (actually performed utterances) are only a minor consideration and the primary focus is, instead, the discursive system underpinning them. This system is different from—but formally like—the *langue* (the language system). Discourse becomes, effectively, a kind of grammar. As we will see, in his *Archaeology of Knowledge* Foucault specifically differentiates his conception of discourse from that of speech act theory and, indeed, from logical analyses which tend to consider language in terms of propositions. Since he is interested in the *conditions* of discourse, Foucault does not mean, by this term, a formal logical, linguistic, or even language-like system.

If formalist approaches to discourse are mostly associated with the discipline of linguistics, 'empirical' approaches, by contrast, largely consist of *sociological* forms of analysis. In this tradition, 'discourse' is frequently taken to mean human conversation. Like certain kinds of formalism, some types of conversational discourse analysis offer formal descriptions of conversational 'texts'. Yet this is not its only—or its main—goal, for it is primarily concerned with the *commonsense knowledges* which ultimately inform conversational rules and procedures. In this respect, empirical approaches to discourse can be seen to share Foucault's concern with discourse in terms of *knowledge*. But, from the outset, it is equally clear that, by 'knowledge', these analysts mean something different from Foucault. In this tradition, 'knowledge' refers to technical knowledge or know-how. For Foucault, 'knowledge' is much more a matter of the social, historical and political conditions under which, for example, statements come to count as true or false.

There is a large range of empirical approaches to discourse analysis. McCarthy (1992) gives a competent summary of what is available in the field at present. But let us take one example: conversation analysis (CA), pioneered by Sacks and based on the ethnomethodological approach to sociology of Garfinkel (1967; Heritage, 1984). Garfinkel offered a critique of American structural-functional sociology which tended to take social facts as given 'things'—pre-formed objects. Coining the term 'ethnomethodology', he believed that his new discipline would be able to ask instead how members of a society rely upon general *methods* in order to actually *accomplish* social facts (Anderson and Sharrock, 1986). But at the same time, Garfinkel also rejected the phenomenological idea that social facts are constructed primarily in consciousness. Like Foucault, he rejected theories which give primacy to a sovereign or originary subject and turned, instead, to overtly *material techniques.*

The difference is that Garfinkel's ethnomethodology set out to *describe* the technical accomplishment of social objects (for example, how are incarcerations brought off?), while Foucault's interest in social techniques is both critical and historical (for example, how do medical discourses during and before the twentieth century produce a particular kind of social subject; how does this limit 'who we can be'; and what strategies are available for broadening or even defeating this limit?).

By the time Sacks came to apply Garfinkel's approach to discourse—mostly in the early 1970s—his central question was even more reliant on descriptions of technique: how are *conversations* (if we consider them as social objects) accomplished by their participants, and is there a set of relatively stable techniques which they use for this? His writings, with colleagues Schegloff and Jefferson, on turn-taking (1974) and on correction (1977) in conversation are the field's classics. Thus most CA work begins with a *corpus* of materials, rather than theoreticist arguments about the mind, cognition or human nature.

Here we can discern a crucial difference between CA and Foucault, whose concept of 'archive' is quite distinct from the idea of an empirical data *corpus.* Foucault's archive is not just a collection of texts or materials (historical documents or transcribed conversations) but the form of organisation of the parts of a discourse (its statements):

> By the word ['archive'], I do not mean the mass of texts which have been collected at a given period, or chanced to have survived oblivion from this period. I mean the set of rules which at a given period and for a definite society defined:
>
> 1) the limits and the forms of *expressibility* . . .
> 2) the limits and the forms of *conservation* . . .
> 3) the limits and the forms of *memory* . . .
> 4) the limits and the forms of *reactivation.* (1978b:14–15)

These limits and forms, of course, refer to the limits and forms of a discursive formation. This is important because, while many of

Foucault's analyses use—like CA—meticulous and detailed textual documentation, this documentation is *not*, in itself, what Foucault means by 'archive'. The documentation and its arrangement by the historian only exist in order to reveal the archive: the conditions (the 'set of rules') by which it is possible to 'know' something at a specific historical point and by which this knowledge changes. Classically, CA's version of discourse looks for techniques of 'saying'—how turns are taken in conversations, for example. By contrast, Foucault's discourse theory looks for techniques of 'what can be said'.

Foucault's rethinking of discourse

Among critical discourse theorists such as Foucault, the term 'discourse' refers not to language or social interaction but to relatively well-bounded areas of social knowledge. And, with exceptions, it is almost impossible to find this use of the term in other—largely Anglo-American—approaches. If our prior conceptions of discourse have been mainly linguistic or sociological ones, we now have to completely rethink the idea. We may even need to be prepared to think of it as a totally different concept in a totally different field which just happens to have the same *name* as something we already know.

According to this new position, in any given historical period we can write, speak or think about a given social object or practice (madness, for example) only in certain specific ways and not others. '*A* discourse' would then be *whatever* constrains—but also enables—writing, speaking and thinking within such specific historical limits. And we deliberately speak of 'a discourse' in the singular: for even though Foucault very frequently uses the mass noun 'discourse', he is typically keen to point out that this is something of a theoretician's shorthand, a way of signalling some common and general properties of discourse*s*. Historically specific discourses (for example, medicine in the nineteenth century) are quite distinct from one another as well as from earlier and later forms of 'themselves' which may or may not have the same names. As we have seen, they are discontinuous.

But they can also overlap and intersect as they change historically, like those discourses on life, labour and language we call bio-medicine, economics and linguistics. Foucault tried to trace these complex comings-together and departures in *The Order of Things* (1970). Sometimes he treats the discourses separately; at other times he looks at their contribution to the possibility of each period having an overall view of the world (which he calls 'the Western episteme'). For example, he finds that, in the sixteenth century, the 'table' of the human sciences had no concepts of life and labour at all. Nor was language thought of as a signifying system or 'medium': it was simply there as 'one of the figurations of the world' (1970:56), a natural device like air and water. Moreover—and this may be difficult for contemporary readers to appreciate—there was no concept of 'Man' or humanity. In fact, Foucault argues that what we *now* call 'humanity' had no way of conceptualising 'its' separateness until the nineteenth century. 'Humanity' is barely a century old! Before this, there were different connections and separations to be made.

The discipline called 'natural history' in the seventeenth and eighteenth centuries was purely descriptive and taxonomic—a taxonomy being a table of types, in this case, of life-forms. These 'scientists' merely collected, described and tabulated species and types; they never tried to form overall theories of life-in-general (as did Darwin in the nineteenth century). Such forms of thought simply weren't available. The same was true of the discourse on labour in these early times. The discipline then known as the 'analysis of wealth' merely tried to examine forms of exchange and trade, as though what we would now think of as humanly produced commodities were 'natural' things to be bought and sold. There was also, at this time, a discourse which dealt with language called 'general grammar'. But just as natural history collected and tabulated species, and the analysis of wealth inspected forms of exchange, so general grammar seemed happy to separate language into nouns and verbs and to examine their types.

By the early nineteenth century, these three discourses had become much more distinct. They had become separate sciences: early biology (whose major figure is Cuvier), early economics (Ricardo) and philological linguistics (Bopp). As the period known as the Enlightenment (Rabinow, 1987:32–50)—and particularly Kant's analysis of the limits or finiteness of what knowledge could achieve—began to have its effect, these separate discourses appeared to have a previously unforeseen object in common: 'Man' as both the one who was able to 'know' and, simultaneously, as the area or object to which knowledge should be applied. It became possible to say that *Man* lives, *Man* labours and *Man* speaks. This makes possible the field of the human sciences—there are new objects which require new analyses—with distinct discourses covering each of the three areas: psychology (human life), sociology (human labour) and the studies of literature and myth (human signification, 'man' to 'man').

Then, in the twentieth century, structuralism announces the 'death of Man': the idea that Man is a fiction, has always been 'really' absent and that what we call 'humanity' is a false construct. With respect to 'life', psychology is replaced by psychoanalysis, which assumes that a uniform structure known as 'the unconscious' inhabits each of us in more or less identical ways. As for 'labour', ethnology now replaces sociology, and structural conditions situate human societies as mere responses (albeit differentiated) to universal conditions and needs. And in the case of 'language', structural linguistics looks for linguistic universals beneath the specific and unique bits of language which are written and spoken. Now contemporary discourses (including, we might add, the discourses on discourse) are put in their historical position. They are relativised or pluralised so that they no longer seem to have unique access to the truth. Truth becomes a function of what *can be* said, written or thought. And Foucault's project becomes one of exposing the historical specificity—the sheer fact that things could have been otherwise (1981:6)—of what we seem to know today with such certainty.

But our more immediate question is: what does Foucault mean by 'discourse'? After working on what he called the discourses of life, labour and language in *The Order of Things*, he immediately began to try to theorise the concept of discourse in his next book, *The Archaeology of Knowledge*. This is perhaps Foucault's most difficult work. *The Order of Things* is complex enough as it is; but to try to read a complicated theoretical reflection on it (which is what *The Archaeology of Knowledge* is), in the absence of *The Order of Things*, is a near impossibility. And still *The Archaeology of*

Knowledge is the main work in which Foucault tries to spell out what he means by 'discourse'. The best way to deal with Foucault's approach to discourse, however, is to work carefully through *The Order of Things* (despite its seemingly arcane history of the human sciences) and then to read *The Archaeology of Knowledge* for a more theoretical formulation of Foucault's rethinking of this topic.

Because the type of 'discourse theory' to which Foucault contributed is less well known in English-speaking circles than formal and empirical approaches, a brief historical preamble is in order. Pre-Foucauldian critical discourse theory originated in continental, largely French, *philosophical* traditions. It had its most cogent application in relation to the history of ideas rather than to formal language systems or social structure. O'Sullivan et al. (1983:72–3) argue that it began with structuralism and its opposition to those 'inherited habits of thought and analysis' which assumed that social and cultural 'objects' existed in the 'real world' ready to be seized or 'adequated'. The structuralists tried to show that, on the contrary, these objects exist only 'as *products*, not *sources*, of . . . signification'. But this position on discourse—which still differs from Foucault's in that it attaches discourse *primarily* to signification—does not mean that 'anything goes'. Because 'objects' are said to be 'discursively produced', this does not imply that we can make the world into anything we want simply by speaking, writing or thinking in a certain way (Macdonell, 1986). Instead structuralist and semiotic approaches to discourse were intended as critiques of individualism and idealism. According to this position, what we can *imagine* (let alone put into practice) is both permitted and constrained by the discursive, that is representational, possibilities at our disposal.

Thus both 'the world' and our consciousness of it are effects of the kinds of representations we can make of it. But, at the same time, discourse is not just a form of representation; it is a *material condition* (or set of conditions) which enables and constrains the socially productive 'imagination'. These conditions can therefore be referred to as 'discourses' or 'discursive conditions of possibility'. The Russian analyst Voloshinov (1973) showed that such discourses (forms of representation) can come into contention and struggle. This struggle is no more clearly seen than in the human sciences themselves (or indeed in the natural sciences) where what Kuhn (1970) calls 'paradigms' may compete for dominance in a particular field. If no case springs to mind immediately, then remember that one may be before us here and now: the case of discourse analysis itself—where what discourse is, and how it is to be analysed—is hotly contended by different approaches.

However, if discourses don't merely represent 'the real', and if in fact they are part of its production, then which discourse is 'best' can't be decided by comparing it with any real object. The 'real' object simply isn't available *for* comparison outside its discursive construction. Instead discourses (forms of representation) might be tested in terms of how they can actually intervene in local struggles. Examples of this kind of highly interventional critical discourse analysis can be found in the work of the anthropologist Michaels (1987) and the co-productions of Australian Aborigines with discourse analysts (Benterrak, Muecke and Roe, 1984). These, to be sure, owe as much to contemporary literary theory as they do to critical discourse theory. At the same time, such interventions cannot afford to neglect a firm theoretical basis—a systematic position on what discourse is and how it works socially and politically. So it is to this that we now turn by looking at how Foucault characterised the 'components' of discourse. Focusing largely on *The Archaeology of Knowledge* (that is, on Foucault's own contribution to discourse theory) we neglect for now the many offshoots and applications of his work in such fields as the history of statistics (Hacking, 1981, 1982), the family (Donzelot, 1980), legal discourse (Wickham, 1987), literary discourse (Williamson, 1989), photography (Tagg, 1988), the body (Turner, 1984) and pedagogy (Luke, 1989).

Foucault argues that formal and empirical approaches have tended to work on the side of the enunciation (*énonciation*) of discourse. By 'enunciation' he means the techniques, the structures, the forms of know-how by which people are able to produce and recognise utterances. Such a narrow focus can include only the surface of language use, the *ways and means by which* concepts and meanings are spoken or written. In place of this emphasis, Foucault (1972) proposes to look at discourses—

specific bodies of knowledge—at the level of the enounc*ed* (*énoncé*) or, as his translators put it, the 'statement'. This change of emphasis moves discourse away from being simply a technical accomplishment (linguistic or interactional) on the part of pre-existing sovereign subjects, and redirects it towards the questions: what can be said? and what can be thought?

Referring back to his historical analyses in *The Order of Things*, Foucault (1972:80) considers his failure there to specify the terms 'discourse' and 'statement' (*énoncé*):

> Instead of gradually reducing the rather fluctuating meaning of the word 'discourse', I believe that I have in fact added to its meanings: treating it sometimes as the general domain of all statements, sometimes as an individualizable group of statements, and sometimes as a regulated practice that accounts for a certain number of statements; and have I not allowed this same word 'discourse', which should have served as a boundary around the term 'statement', to vary as I shifted my analysis or its point of application, as the statement itself faded from view?

To clear up this confusion, Foucault asks whether we could think of the statement as a *unit of (a) discourse*, just as the sentence is a unit of (a) language. If so, it is then necessary to ask what kind of unit it is. For example, would it be exactly the *same* as a proposition, a sentence or a speech act? Let us take these in order.

First, a statement cannot be the same as a proposition. The proposition is the basic unit of logical analysis: a declarative utterance describing an actual state of affairs, or else a 'truism'. Taking Foucault's (1972:81) own example, the propositions 'No one heard' and 'It is true that no one heard' have identical 'contents'—to all intents and purposes they are the same proposition—but may constitute two different statements. We can see this by asking what they *state* in particular circumstances. If each were to occur as the first line of a novel, Foucault continues, they would set up different kinds of narrative. The first—'No one heard'—could be 'an observation made either by the author, or by a character', while the second 'can only be in a group of statements constituting an interior monologue, a silent discussion with oneself, or a fragment of dialogue, a group of questions or answers' (1972:81).

According to this, Foucault's first criterion for a statement is that it should be responsive to what Pêcheux (1975) calls 'functioning'. Propositional content, at least in traditional logics, is thought to remain constant across different local usages. But unlike propositions, statements—as components of discursive formations—have to be thought of primarily as *functional* units. They do things, bring about effects rather than merely 'represent' states of affairs.

Secondly, Foucault argues, a statement is not the same as a sentence; at least as far as we can tell. Truncated 'sentences'—such as 'Absolutely!'—can, it is true, carry the force of statements. They can do things, create effects. But this objection is trivial. Even formalist approaches acknowledge that such truncations can count as sentences. In fact the sentence (according to the various schools of linguistics) is itself very difficult to define. And so we will never be in a position to decide clearly one way or another about the correspondence (or lack of it) between sentences and Foucault's statements. But there is some relatively firm ground. For it *is* possible to say that certain word groupings which are clearly *not* sentences do carry the force of statements. Foucault's (1972:82) example is the paradigm of the Latin verb *amare*: *amo*, *amas*, *amat* . . . which schoolchildren once had to recite in class. Obviously—perhaps even by definition—this is not a sentence, for it lists the forms which can 'fill slots' (verb positions) in actual sentences. Yet it is a statement, a 'statement of the different personal inflections of the . . . verb'. Thus classificatory schemata, tables, maps and taxonomies, though rarely expressed as sentences, can be statements. The periodic table of the elements is a statement and so is a price schedule.

More importantly, these examples show clearly how groups of statements (discourses) act to both constrain and enable what we can know. Statements, that is, cannot be characterised by their syntactic or grammatical forms. Expressions which *do not use verbal language* can be statements: 'a graph, a growth curve, an age pyramid, a distribution cloud . . .' (1972:82). The important thing (and this is Foucault's second criterion for a statement) is that statements should be parts of knowledge.

Thirdly, a statement cannot be the same as a speech act. This is because some—but not all—speech acts require *more than a single statement* in order to be 'felicitous' in Austin's (1975) sense. Austin argued that speech acts (for example, saying 'I do' in a wedding ceremony—an utterance which accomplishes an event in and by its very saying), in order to be successful, must meet certain 'felicity conditions'. Not all instances of 'I do' will count: it must be said in front of someone who is vested with the authority to conduct marriages, the two parties must consent, and so on. It is true that both Austin's speech acts and Foucault's statements can be said to 'accomplish' events and create effects. But equivalences between (some) speech acts and (some) statements are merely coincidental.

Can we say, for instance, that there is equivalence between 'I promise' (when it is said as a proposal of marriage within the *discourse* of mediaeval romance) and 'I promise' (when it is said as an agreement to meet for lunch)? Perhaps these are equivalent speech acts (strictly, they are both 'commissives'), but each is a different statement. The two statements occur in totally different social 'technologies' and historically formed discursive practices. Each, if successful, produces distinct individual human subjects: lovers and lunchers; each, again if successful, (re)creates and maintains political institutions as different as love and lunch! Hence the third criterion for a statement is that it should be part of a technique or techniques for the production of human subjects and institutions.

Returning to Foucault's initial question about whether statements are perhaps 'units' of discourses, we can see that the answer is a qualified 'no'. A statement is not *strictly* a unit at all in the way that the proposition, the sentence and the speech act are. Instead, it is a 'function that operates vertically in relation to these various units, and which enables one to say of a series of signs whether or not they are present in it' (1972:86). It is 'not itself a unit, but a function that cuts across a domain of structures and possible unities, and which reveals them, with concrete contents, in time and space' (1972:87). Statements can therefore be understood, not as fixed components, but only via the *rules* which govern their functioning. But these rules are not like grammatical rules; they have to do with historically variable bodies of knowledge; they are the rules for what it is possible to know. Hence they are not susceptible to (nor can they help us arrive at) a general theory of *language*.

Statements and the rules which govern them are not purely linguistic (indeed, we have seen that they can be completely non-linguistic), nor are they purely material but, in fact, connect these two domains. In order to analyse or describe discursive rules, we must always turn to specific historical conditions—to the piecemeal, the local and the contingent. Events, no matter how specific, cannot happen just anyhow. They must happen according to certain constraints, rules or conditions of possibility. And these mean that discourses always function in relation to *power relations* in Foucault's sense, which is the central topic of our next chapter. Because power is crucial to any understanding of Foucault's theory of discourse, we must consider it here briefly—if prematurely. For Foucault, 'power' is very different from traditional socio-political conceptions of it. Discourse is not a mere effect or end-product of pre-existing Power (with a capital 'P'). Nor is power 'owned' by some privileged person or group and exercised 'simply as an obligation or a prohibition on those who "do not have it"' (Foucault, 1977a:27). Power, for Foucault, is not just the ruthless domination of the weaker by the stronger (to paraphrase Nietzsche); in fact, it is not to be 'had' at all.

> Power is everywhere; not because it embraces everything but because it comes from everywhere . . . Power comes from below; that is there is no binary and all-encompassing opposition between ruler and ruled at the root of power relations, and serving as a general matrix—no such duality extending from the top down and reacting on more and more limited groups to the very depths of the social body. One must suppose rather that the manifold relations of force that take shape and come into play in the machinery of production, in families, limited groups and institutions, are the basis for wide-ranging effects of cleavage that run through the social body as a whole. (Foucault, 1979a:93–4)

Eco (1986:244), however, argues that this radical rethinking of power by Foucault does not mean that it has *no* possible connections with language. Instead, Foucault's

> image of power closely recalls the idea of the system that linguists call *the given language*. The given language is, true,

> coercive (it forbids me to say 'I are him', under pain of being incomprehensible), but its coercion doesn't derive from an individual decision, or from some center that sends out rules in all directions: It is a social product, it originates as a constrictive apparatus precisely through general assent . . . I'm not sure we can say that a given language is a device of power . . . but it is surely a model of power. (Italics added)

So as an illustration of how far we have come now from formalist conceptions of discourse-as-language, we can now see that the linguistic system (the *langue*) itself, far from being the source of discourse, is just one instance of power where power is considered as a set of *relations* of force. Because these relations are local and historically contingent, they cannot be 'predicted' by a general theory. Only particular investigations—what Foucault calls 'archaeological' investigations, investigations of an 'archive'—can specify them.

Returning to the level of the statement: statements are best approached, not individually, but in terms of the organisations or archives of which they form a part. Hence what can be said or not said about something is neither absolutely fixed (because it varies historically) nor is it open to the whims of the moment. For

> the archive . . . determines that all these things said do not accumulate endlessly in an amorphous mass, nor are they inscribed in an unbroken linearity, nor do they disappear at the mercy of chance external accidents; but they are grouped together in distinct figures, composed together in accordance with multiple relations, maintained or blurred in accordance with specific regularities. (1972:128)

Even though it can (by chance) take a linguistic form, the statement is a socio-historical function rather than a strictly linguistic one. Yet because statements can *still be located in talk and texts*, we can work from collections of statements to their organising archives. This archaeological method shows that social histories of thought, knowledge and power are both unique and specific as well as having general properties. Foucault (1981) called this method of tracing the systematic (archival) properties of unique and local affairs 'eventalisation'. It is no accident, then, that he refers to the archive as 'the very root of the statement-*event*' (1972:129 italics added).

But Foucault's idea of the discursive archive does not simply replace concepts like 'system', 'structure', '*langue*' and so on. Rather, analyses of an archive as a condition of 'stating', as a relatively stable system of functioning (at specific places and times), must be taken together with analyses of its historical flux, of 'the general system of the formation and transformation of statements' (1972:130). 'Archive' is a much more mobile and fluid term than the relatively fixed concept of 'episteme' (1970). The concept of an archive 'deprives us of our continuities' (1972:131) and establishes the fact that human subjects and historical events are not firm and discrete (id)entities but are fragmented and changing *sites* across which the flows of power move. The archive, more radically, 'establishes that we are difference, that our reason is the difference of discourses, our history the history of difference, our selves the difference of masks' (1972:131).

We have seen already how Foucault uses this method to analyse the case of Pierre Rivière (1978a). This case is interesting because it concerns a particularly unstable situation in which different forms of discourse on punishment came into conflict and difference over the nature of a crime, a multiple murder. Different forms of power contested the right to say what Rivière *was*: was he a cunning criminal on whose body retribution had to be delivered, or a madman suffering from the disease of monomania, and requiring 'treatment'? This type of discourse analysis, then, has intimate connections with how human subjects are formed, how institutions attempt to 'normalise' persons on the margins of social life, how historical conditions of knowledge change and vary—how things 'weren't as necessary as all that', as Foucault (1981:6) once put it. In short, it is intimately bound to the field of politics. In the next section we will look at how Foucault's conception of discourse opens up a number of political possibilities via a detailed look at his 1966 paper 'Politics and the Study of Discourse' (1978b), which originated as an interview.

Discourse and politics

To use a very rough and ready equation, it looks as if, for Foucault, discourses are knowledges; knowledges are collected into disciplines; and the disciplines which are his main concern are those of the human sciences (psychiatry, medicine, economics and linguistics in particular—if we consider the works up to and including *The Archaeology of Knowledge*). If this is true, then isn't Foucault's work just an academic commentary on academic knowledge—a metacommentary which is useful only to a very limited group of specialists? And if this is also true, then doesn't our claim that Foucault's work is 'critical' seem equally limited? Doesn't it seem as if it could never make any difference to the world outside the academy, to politics in the broad sense, let alone to a 'progressive' politics? But behind this question lies a problem with a long history of its own: what *is* the relation between academic disciplines generally and the broad social, political and historical areas 'outside' them?

Foucault's rather novel answer to this last question has important consequences for the previous question about the use of his *own* discourse for (or its connections with) a progressive or interventional politics. Yet the way the question is put to him in 'Politics and the Study of Discourse' (1978b) makes it look as if his own view of interventional possibilities is rather pessimistic. If the historical flow of ideas is radically *discontinuous* and also part of a '*system*', then aren't we left in a rather difficult situation: either to accept the system, or submit to the chaotic and random changes brought about by discontinuity? This is how the interviewer puts the question to Foucault:

> Doesn't a thought which introduces discontinuity and the constraint of a system into the history of the mind remove all basis for a progressive political intervention? Does it not lead to the following dilemma:
>
> —either the acceptance of the system,
>
> —or the appeal to an uncontrolled event, to the irruption of exterior violence which alone is capable of upsetting the system? (1978b:8)

Foucault first argues that the phrase 'introduc[ing] discontinuity and the constraint of a system into the history of the mind' needs to be reconsidered before it can properly apply to his own project. Secondly, with the corrections to the question duly made, he then tries to show how his rethinking of 'man's' position in (discursive or disciplinary) history can be crucial for a progressive politics. Let us deal with each of these in turn.

First, the idea of a single system has to be pluralised into 'systems'. What are Foucault's reasons for this? He says openly that he is a pluralist and that his problem is the individualisation of discourses. These specific discourses or disciplines must not be looked at as a global entity (discourse in general) because their histories are quite distinct. Some disciplines have a long histories (medicine and mathematics), while others do not (economics and psychiatry). Furthermore, within each of these fields of knowledge, the statements which compose them are not only distinct in each case but also subject to quite different kinds of *transformation*, if (and as) we examine their historical course in sufficient detail. In the case of any discourse, it's impossible to find a single and unique principle 'behind' these local transformations. To search for such a principle is to misunderstand discursive change. There are two standard ways of undertaking such a task, and each is equally mistaken in Foucault's view.

The first recourse he calls 'historical-transcendental'. Here the discourse is assumed to have an original foundation, an absolute centre (rather like Newton's universe); but it is never reached or regained, and each successive historical 'stage' of the discipline can only approximate it. This approach is illusory because it tries to restore a non-existent totality to a series of what are actually local and specific transformations. The second recourse he calls 'empirical or psychological': here the discourse is assumed to have been founded by an actual person (as, for example, Comte is often called 'the father of sociology'). The task of the historian of ideas is then to find this founder's supposedly real intentions 'behind' his texts. This intention (or, more abstractly, 'genius') underpins all the successive changes within the discourse, so that what may happen within a discipline at a given moment can always be referred back to this (now silent and forgotten) 'mind'. The historian's task is akin to unravelling a thread (or many threads), back to the originary 'person' who set it (or them) in motion. Both of these approaches fail to 'individualise' or 'eventalise' the discipline in question. In order to work counter to them, Foucault sets out the various criteria by which to examine discourses in their specificity.

Any discourse may be seen to have a number of components which are fairly easily identifiable: *objects* (the things they study or produce), *operations* (the methods and techniques or 'ways of treating' these objects), *concepts* (terms and ideas which are routinely found in the discipline and which may constitute its unique language) and *theoretical options* (those different assumptions, theories and perhaps even hypotheses available within the discipline, and which might oblige physicists, say, to 'decide' between relativity theory and quantum mechanics). This four-part division is important as a first approximation. When we look at specific instances of disciplines, however, we find that their objects are quite diffuse and scattered; that their operations are hard to trace in terms of their 'succession' from an earlier period; and that their concepts and theoretical options may be incompatible or incommensurate with one another. Instead, Foucault argues that a discourse is identified by the existence of criteria of *formation*, *transformation*, and *correlation* (of objects, concepts, etc.). He sees his archaeology as the discourse which discovers such sets of criteria or rules. The rules of formation are the conditions which make possible in the first place the objects and concepts of a discourse. The rules of transformation are the limits of its capacities to modify itself, the 'threshold' from which it can bring new rules 'into play'. The rules of correlation are the 'ensemble of relations' which a discourse has with other discourses at a given time and with the 'nondiscursive context' in which it finds itself.

By looking for these criteria or rules as the socially local and historically delimited 'objects' of his *own* discourse, Foucault argues that he is able to 'substitute differentiated analyses for the themes of a totalising history ("the progress of reason" or "the spirit of a century")' (1978b:10). This view of history as a general 'medium' of human 'development' which is guided by a master hidden hand is the legacy, he argues, of the nineteenth century.

Instead of a single essential history, then, Foucault proposes innumerable histories: histories of distinct and different discourses in terms of their transformations and retentions. And in place of the 'grand underlying theory' or 'spirit', he suggests that the various discourses of a period may form an 'episteme'—though later he drops this term as unnecessary to the analysis. The episteme is not a theme which unites the different discourses: rather it is the space they inhabit, which 'is a space of *dispersion* . . . an *open field of relationships*' (1978b:10). Hence instead of imagining a single and essential historical principle acting in a shadowy way 'behind' each period (sometimes called the *Weltanschauung*, the *Zeitgeist* or the 'spirit of the times'), Foucault posits the episteme as a non-unified, multiple and complex field of play. Then, rather tantalisingly, he adds: 'wherever I have deemed it necessary I have allowed the *systems* to proliferate' (1978b:11).

Secondly, the idea of a single type of discontinuity has to be pluralised into 'discontinuities'. If Foucault's discourse analysis is to deal with very different types of disciplinary transformation, then it must reject theories of historical change which retain the idea of a 'deeper' continuity commonly called 'tradition, influence, habits of thought, broad mental forms, [or] constraints of the human mind' (1978b:11). At the same time, it is not going to look for the source of these transformations inside the heads and minds of unique individuals and (mis)describe it as 'the genius of great inventors, crises of conscience, [or] the appearance of a new form of mind'. The transformations Foucault speaks of are not merely incidental to historical change but actually *constitute* it. There is no other place to look for the 'reasons' behind the changes.

Foucault then argues that there are three main 'places' where one can find discursive or disciplinary change. First, one can look *within* the discourse to its own *derivations*. Here he gives many examples from the ancient discourse of general grammar. The flavour of his remarks can be summed up by saying, for example, that a discipline will bring to bear operations which have normally applied to one of its objects and then apply it to another, thereby altering the character of the analysis of the second object. In physics, a famous example is the extension of the discovery of sound waves to the study of light; then, by a further extension, if sound waves are propagated in a medium (for example air or water) then so too must light waves (Hesse, 1962). From this arose a new physical medium, the ether, in which light is supposed to move. Interestingly enough, because no empirical equivalent of this hypothetical medium could be found, a whole set of changes in basic physical assumptions (the supposed 'relativistic revolution') had to be made in order to rethink the idea of light as *both* particle and wave, and thus cope with the 'failure' of the derivation from sound.

Secondly, the historian can look at the *mutations* of a discourse. Its boundaries may alter: for example, how is it that the discipline of statistics changed its 'unit' of analysis from the hearth to the head (from the household to the individual) at a quite specific point (Hacking, 1981)? The subject who operates within a discourse, or on whom the discourse operates, may alter positions: for example (here we use Foucault's own), the eighteenth-century naturalist gives up 'listening, interpreting, deciphering'—and all of the various positions associated with deduction—and becomes a *looker*. Sight becomes the primary instrument of a new inductive mode, and from that time operations are conducted according to visual perceptions. The language of the discourse—and note how far we have come now from the *self-identity* of language and discourse—may begin to operate in a different way. As Freudian approaches to psychiatric analysis emerged, for example, language was no longer simply a way of recording or representing the analyst's findings; it became instead one of the means by which those findings were arrived at. The patient's language became the central key to his or her dreams, and thus to the unconscious drives 'behind' it. Or again: the 'places' of the discourse in terms of broader social relations may alter. Think here of the establishment of hospitals and clinics (and the different functions of these over time) or of prisons and schools. What the discourse does, whom it acts upon, how it is distributed, and the forms of resistance it meets (if any) are all open to transformation.

Thirdly, there will be broader transformations (called 'redistributions') that occur between two or more discourses. During the 1960s, for example, general sociology was arguably the most important and relied-upon discourse for social analysis. By our own times it has fragmented into different 'schools' and gone into decline; it is now less important than economics, industrial psychology and a whole range of other specialisms within the social sciences. Positions in discursive hierarchies can change, with one discourse taking over the relatively supreme position of another. Again, we tend to think that the discourses of the natural sciences are now (and have always been) superior to those of the social sciences. And indeed we can think of the ways in which the concepts of the natural sciences have been brought over into social analysis: Foucault himself notes how nineteenth-century biological concepts were imported into sociology and linguistics (which is why Durkheim, for example, was able to think of society as an 'organism'). But this relationship between science and the social sciences can be reversed: think of how terms like 'genetic code', 'genetic information' and 'messenger RNA' as used in genetics have been taken from linguistics and information theory. And lastly we can see that a theory once exclusive to one discipline can be dropped and taken over by another. Foucault instances the 'theory of the continuity of beings', which transfers from philosophy to the natural sciences in the nineteenth century. But we could also mention a range of other instances in the humanities. For example, hardly anyone but a Jungian psychologist would nowadays use Jung's theory of archetypes (the idea of eternal mythic themes existing behind every specific cultural manifestation); yet the theory is still to be encountered in American 'myth criticism' as a means of finding archetypal 'connections' between ancient and modern authors who could not have 'known' each other.

Foucault, therefore, argues against his interlocutor that he is not examining discontinuity in general but a whole range of specific discontinuit*ies* between and within discourses. Four things are important to him in studying these quite different *kinds* of discontinuity. First, he does not want to use them to derive an overall theory of change or, indeed, merely to make up a 'list of innovations'; rather he wants to describe, analytically, some very specific transformations. Secondly, he does not want his analysis to be confused with a 'psychological diagnosis' of the great scientific innovators. It does not matter to him what happens under their skulls because this, too, is only one of the products (not the causes) of those discursive conditions of possibility we have called 'rules' or 'criteria'. Thirdly, he does not want to think of these discursive transformations as merely superficial, behind which is 'an all-powerful subject which manipulates them' (1978b:13). Discourse is not simply the means by which a human subject—existing prior to the discourse—expresses itself or accomplishes something. Rather, the discursive conditions (rules and criteria) set up specific places or positions in which subjects can form as, for example, 'patients', 'doctors', 'perverts', 'schizophrenics', 'criminals' and so on. Fourthly, instead of these almost dominant obsessions of the humanities and social sciences, Foucault wants to describe and analyse the *dependencies* that exist *within* discourses (between their objects and operations), *between* discourses (such as the complex relations between the discourses on life, labour and language analysed in *The Order of Things*) and *between* discourses and the broader forms of socio-political change in which they arise.

To this extent, then, discontinuity is not a single principle: 'there is absolutely no question of substituting a category of the "discontinuous" for the no less abstract and general one of the "continuous"' (1978b:13). The fact that Foucault gave up trying to find underlying causes or great minds behind historical changes does not mean that something so fixed as discontinuity-in-general (an *essence* of discontinuity) has to fill the space they have vacated. Why, indeed, can't the centre be empty?

If historical change were to have a single cause, then we would indeed be doomed to ineffectiveness. On this deterministic view of things, human subjects would have no scope to alter the conditions in which they find themselves. Again, if historical change merely emanated from the mind, then all who have minds could simply 'think' their way out of the conditions around them. On this idealistic view of things, there would be no need for a progressive politics: we would be in an eternal state of progress, for liberty would be our natural condition. Both positions are equally flawed in terms of political strategies: and so it is appropriate that Foucault should abandon them. He does not reject continuity (as a historical principle) for purely philosophical reasons, though there are good philosophical reasons for doing so; rather, he rejects it *because* the politics of continu*ism* are conservative since they appeal, ultimately, either to unmovable causes or natural liberties.

Thirdly, the idea of a 'history of the mind' has to be replaced by a history of discourse. Here Foucault imagines his interlocutor returning to a simple distinction between thought and language, as if this distinction exhausted the possibilities of a history of ideas. On this view, if Foucault is not interested in discourse-as-language, then he *must* be interested in discourse-as-thought: 'the intention of the men who have formulated [the texts], the meanings which, voluntarily or unknowingly, they have deposited therein' (1978b:14). Indeed, Foucault agrees, he is not interested in any discourse's system of *language*, but in the rules and criteria for the transformation of statements—and yet there is no reason to suppose that these rules and criteria are someone's personal thoughts. As Foucault remarks time after time, 'the consciousness, obscure or explicit, of speaking subjects' (1978b:14) is not what is behind the historical transformations which are his proper object. Such transformations go collectively (for a particular discourse) by the name of its 'archive', whose various *limits* may be enumerated as *expressibility*, *conservation* and so on. From this there follow three recommendations which (if anything is) are probably at the 'heart' of Foucauldian thinking:

> 1) Treat past discourse not as a theme for a *commentary* which would revive it, but as a *monument* to be described in its character-disposition.
>
> 2) Seek in the discourse not its laws of construction, as do the structural methods, but its conditions of existence.
>
> 3) Refer the discourse not to the thought, to the mind or to the subject which might have given rise to it, but to the practical field in which it is deployed. (1978b:15)

If these general maxims hold, then the original question asked of Foucault would now refer to his introduction of 'the diversity of *systems* and the play of *discontinuities* into the history of *discourses*' (1978b:15). 'System' and 'discontinuity' are pluralised and dispersed; 'mind' is deleted and displaced by 'discourse'. But then there is the second part of the question: what does this pluralist, discontinuist and anti-mentalist position have to do with a progressive politics?

With regard to this crucial question, Foucault offers two sets of answers. The first has to do with critique, namely the 'critical *operations*' which he has undertaken in his own field of study, roughly, the history of ideas. The second concerns 'the realm of *objects*' which his discourse deals with, or 'attempts to bring out', and its connection with political intervention in the wider sense. Let us deal with these in order.

Foucault offers four types of *critical operation* performed by his variety of discourse analysis on traditionalist approaches to the history of ideas: the establishment of limits; the elimination of binary oppositions; the critique of discourse as a restricted historical domain; and the establishment of a more certain status for the history of ideas. Taking the first operation first: traditional approaches, he argues, have given themselves a 'limitless space' in which to operate; and in place of this he wants to establish limits. He offers three principal challenges to this supposed limitlessness.

- Instead of thinking of discourse (in the singular) as a global 'language' pertaining to a global history, so that everything (even silence) refers back to a hidden 'meaning' which the historian must find and interpret, Foucault argues that discourses (in the plural) are 'limited practical domains' (1978b:16) which have their own 'rules of formation' and 'conditions of existence'. There is no metadiscourse, or higher discourse, which grounds specific discourses.
- Instead of thinking that a totally free and unlimited human subject merely 'uses' the techniques of discourse to express itself, that is, to construct meanings, Foucault argues that the historian of ideas can find, as part and parcel of a discourse, 'the operations exercised by different "discoursing" subjects' (1978b:16). This is just one constituent of discourse analysis (as history of ideas). It gives no priority or privilege to the human subject, although it does not, as in severe versions of structuralism, 'delete' the subject (Althusser, 1976). In fact, in his later work, Foucault went on to give detailed attention to those *discursive* operations which he called 'the techniques of the self'.

- Instead of thinking that history once had a definite origin so deeply buried in the past that we have lost touch with it, so that we must now remember it afresh as the 'real' starting point and purpose of humanity's 'being in the world', Foucault suggests that history is differentiated and fragmented into particular discourses, and that each fragment (each discourse) has a threshold, a process of birth and an equally complex process of disappearance which can be analysed and described.

All of these mistaken views of history stem from nineteenth-century philosophy, which relied on an essential historical origin, a psychological version of the subject (as 'consciousness') and the idea of hidden meanings. These assumptions or 'themes' have entered into a whole range of twentieth-century disciplines, on both sides of the so-called humanities/sciences divide. Foucault regards his challenge to this trinity of mistaken assumptions as liberating in its own right.

The second critical operation is the elimination of 'ill-considered' oppositions. Here Foucault gives a long list of binary distinctions which the history of ideas has used as its stock-in-trade. Reducing these to three we get: tradition versus innovation; ordinary versus special knowledge (genius); stability versus crisis. By a further process of reduction, we can see that the first term of each pair refers to history-as-fixed and the second to history-as-mobile. It is as if the historian's job were merely the documentation of periods of stasis and dynamism—original/traditional history (the assertion of the origin), and sudden bursts of rethinking or overturning inspired by great 'revolutionary' minds. Foucault argues instead that both simultaneity (the study of fixed points in time) and succession (the study of historical change) are subject to difference: 'I undertake to relate the history of perpetual difference' (1978b:17). History is to be freed from yet another trinity, this time of metaphors: the evolutionist metaphor of regress and progress; the biological metaphor of death and life; the dynamic metaphor of fixity and movement. None of these 'great themes' is able to account for historical specificity and difference.

Foucault's third critical operation works against this denial of specificity as it applies particularly to *discourse*. It is true that historians of ideas have had a place for discourse, but usually as a secondary concept only, always subject to a more essential historical theme. Discourse has been treated

- as language: purely as a medium of expression, the surface representation of 'deeper' abstract thoughts
- as individual psychology: the property of some unique individual, or else as the 'styles' or 'themes' employed by an individual
- as a mere adjunct to 'the mind': so that 'the operations are all carried out prior to discourse' (1978b:17).

These positions seem to turn discourse into 'nothing or almost nothing' (1978b:18), a mere surface effusion of something much more profound. They forget that they too are discourses, and that the 'something much more profound' is always their effect or product rather than their 'real' foundation. In simply saying what 'is' (and then adding on discourse as the technique of its expression), traditional histories of ideas want to deny discourses and statements ('things said') any kind of fundamental role in the processes of history. Foucault wishes to restore that role.

Hence his fourth critical operation, the upshot of the previous three, involves '*freeing from their uncertain status* this ensemble of disciplines which we call history of ideas'. This traditional uncertainty stems, of course, from a reliance on such immaterial foundational concepts as 'spirit of the times', 'genius', 'ultimate origin' and so on, and it takes a number of forms. First, the history of ideas has no sharp boundaries or points of beginning or ending: almost anything can be made to fit into its territory. Secondly, these historical disciplines are uncertain as to their proper *object*, which can vary from 'mental forms', 'consciousness', the 'characteristic features shared by men of one period' (1978b:18) and so on through an indefinitely long list. Thirdly, even when the history of ideas can arrive at 'facts', there is little agreement on how these ought to be linked to other historical realms 'outside' the realm of ideas. Some historians see ideas merely as a reflection or a refraction of 'real' (non-ideal) historical conditions; others, on the contrary, see ideas as actually determining other historical formations (such as politics, economy, cultural production, and so on).

By rethinking the concept of discourse as designating not merely knowledges and disciplines, but also *transformable units of history*, Foucault effectively establishes for the history of ideas a clear and distinct 'object' which does not have to be analysed by reference to 'extrinsic conditions' (1978b:19). Instead, Foucault argues, one can do history of ideas purely and simply as an analysis of the conditions *intrinsic* to actual discourses. This reduces the amorphousness of the discipline (history of ideas) while increasing its analytic complexity.

So much then for the forms of intervention Foucault claims to make from *within* his own discipline. What now of its extension 'outwards' in the direction of political thinking more generally? Foucault begins his analysis of this problem by asking whether a progressive politics would be best served by a pre-Foucauldian history of ideas and its nebulous idealism, or, on the contrary, by its 'meticulous destruction' (1978b:19) and replacement by a more specific and materialist analysis. For how can one base a progressive politics on a mythical 'primitive foundation' (such as a fixed and static 'human nature') or on a 'global history of totalities' (1978b:20), seeing that neither of these offers any room for manoeuvre? On the other hand, can we call a politics 'progressive' if it gives primary value to a free-ranging and unconstrained human consciousness? For in that case any and every avenue of change and intervention would be open to human subjects. By contrast with these options (determinism and idealism), Foucault's discourse analysis at least offers a way of *calculating strategies* for historical transformation. Hence the centrality of Foucault's rethinking of history as discourse(s) for political practice. In this context, let's take a crucial passage from Foucault:

> There exists today a problem which is not without importance for political practice: the problem of the status, of the conditions of existence, of functioning, of the institutionalizing of scientific discourses. That's what I have undertaken to analyze historically—by choosing the discourses which have, not the strongest epistemological structure (mathematics or physics), but the densest and most complex field of positivity (medicine, economics, the human sciences). (1978b:20)

By 'positivity' Foucault is indicating here that these discourses are 'practices linked to certain conditions, obedient to certain rules, and susceptible to certain transformations' (1978b:25). His discursive objects (the disciplines of the human sciences) are clearly forms of social practice which have wide-ranging effects on society generally. Who, for example, has not been affected by the massive changes within medical science since the 1960s—not just its 'discoveries' and 'innovations' but also and more importantly its attention to new objects (diet, sexuality, addiction); its changed modes of operation (towards methods of prevention in whole populations as opposed to curing individual bodies); its conceptual shifts (in the case of mental illnesses, from notions of cause relating to family and environment towards etiologies in neuro-chemical functioning); the alterations in its theoretical options (viral theories of cancer, theories of cancer related to 'lifestyle', 'stress', 'pollution', 'ozone depletion' and so on). An interventional politics might want to ask whether individuals and populations should simply comply with such 'characterisations' of their bio-functions by giving over 'knowledge of themselves' to medicalised knowledges. If they should not, then there is a question concerning the calculation of strategies of intervention. But how can such strategies be arrived at if their 'calculators' are ignorant of the rules and criteria—*within* the discourse of medicine—for its own historical transformation?

Hence political practice cannot simply 'transgress' or 'overthrow' disciplinary formations. Historically it never has done: 'political practice did not transform the meaning or form of the discourse, but the conditions of its emergence, insertion and functioning; it transformed the mode of existence of medical discourse' (1978b:21). At this point Foucault lists a range of such political operations which were crucial for the formation of medical discourse early in the nineteenth century. These include the political specification of who had the legal right to practice; which institutions should be created to manage medicine; the forms of economy necessary for its survival (for example, allowing one's body to be used as a medical specimen in return for treatment); which publications could properly disseminate medical knowledge; how medicine should be administered, regulated and controlled. These overtly political moves do not work upon the objects, concepts, operations, etc., of medicine; rather they 'modify its rules of formation' (1978b:22).

There is similarly no need for theoretical speculation on whether political *practice* 'reflects', 'translates' or 'expresses' medical *ideas* (1978b:22), for the relation between politics and medicine does not take place at this level. Surprisingly, the relation can be much more direct since, according to Foucault's early analyses (1967, 1970, 1973), political practice has always intervened historically at the level of the rules of formation of a discourse. The relations between political practice and social/disciplinary techniques can be 'very direct', 'since they no longer have to pass through the consciousness of speaking subjects nor through the efficacity of thought' (1978b:22).

So, coming back to the initial question, Foucault's discourse analysis is by no means politically pessimistic. When historical changes occur, they are 'not arbitrary nor "free"' (1978b:23). Rather they are forms of calculation which cannot be given over either to some kind of abstract 'discontinuity' (historical chaos) or to an equally abstract historical 'purposiveness'. And Foucault offers some reasonably direct (if analytically arduous) methods and operations for performing such calculations. That is why he writes directly against the characterisation of his work as nothing more than an isolated academic specialism:

> I am not just amusing myself by making the game more complicated for a few lively minds. I am trying to define in what way, to what extent, to what level discourses, and particularly scientific discourses, can be objects of a political practice, and in what system of dependency they can be in relation to it. (1978b:23)

And finally, he offers a fivefold characterisation of what a progressive politics is, showing in each case how his counter-theory of the history of discourses reaches the parts which others cannot. This is worth quoting at length.

> —A progressive politics is one which recognizes the historical conditions and the specified rules of a practice, whereas other politics recognize only ideal necessities, univocal determinations, or the free play of individual initiative.

—A progressive politics is one which defines in a practice the possibilities of transformation and the play of dependencies between these transformations, whereas other politics rely on the uniform abstraction of change or the thaumaturgical presence of genius.
—A progressive politics does not make man or consciousness or the subject in general into a universal operator of all transformations: it defines the different levels and functions which subjects can occupy in a domain which has its own rules of formation.
—A progressive politics does not consider that discourses are the result of mute processes or the expression of a silent consciousness; but rather that—whether as science, or literature or religious statements, or political discourses—they form a practice which is articulated upon the other practices.
—A progressive politics does not find itself with respect to the scientific discourses, in a position of 'perpetual demand' or of 'sovereign criticism,' but must know the manner in which diverse scientific discourses, in their positivity . . . are part of a system of correlations with other practices. (1978b:25)

If we reduce this to its most basic constituents, we can say that what connects discourses—and their analysis—with politics is the whole field of *power* and the positions it generates for *subjects.* How Foucault deals with these two concepts is the substance of our next two chapters.

3

Power

This chapter investigates in some detail Foucault's retheorisation of the concept of power, the critical importance of which cannot be overstated. It shifts the focus of political analysis away from relations of production or signification to a study of *power* relations. For Foucault, the question of subjection, and the political struggles associated with 'identities', constitute the most important issues of our time. Political practice therefore cannot be separated from the fundamental philosophical question of 'being' or 'subjectivity'. By studying subjection in terms of its imbrication within power relations, Foucault was unrivalled in drawing out the full political and historical dimensions of this philosophical concern.

Although it is clear that Foucault's focus on the question of power constitutes such a shift in the direction of his thinking as to form the basis of many critical evaluations of his work as a whole, it is also the case that Foucault's writings on power cannot be discussed outside his investigations of the production of 'truth', and of what this implies for the status of human subjects in contemporary societies. Foucault's conception of discourse is indispensable for an understanding of the role of 'power' in the production of knowledge—including, importantly, *self*-knowledge. Indeed, when some commentators discuss Foucault's conception of power, they often do so by leaving aside the relationship of power to the historical production of truth. We consider this unsatisfactory, and hope to do justice to the radical nature of Foucault's thesis on power by highlighting the essential link between power relations and their capacity to 'produce' the truths we live by.

In many western societies today, 'truth' is seen as the product of science or scientific 'methods'. It is all very well to be 'sceptical' of science. But it is much more difficult to pose adequately the question of *why* sciences are held in such high esteem. Foucault's work as a whole moves some way towards formulating this question. It does this by challenging the status not of the truths generated by sciences but of the *conditions* necessary for their production. While the 'natural' sciences can claim a certain epistemological rigour independently of other social factors or historical forces (physics and mathematics are the examples often cited here), Foucault is interested only in the truths generated by much less credible or 'unglamorous' systems of knowledge. The systems of knowledge Foucault scrutinises imply immediate and solid connections to social relations: economics, medicine, and the 'human sciences'. These are 'sciences', but unlike mathematics they can function as sciences only by relying on the 'densest and most complex field of positivity' (1978b:20). Thus the conditions required for the production of truth within these knowledges are much less stable and far more difficult to control. Yet, somewhat disturbingly perhaps, these are also the knowledges most quick to pronounce truths about human nature, human potential, human endeavour, and the future of the human condition in general.

In his earlier studies, such as *The Birth of the Clinic* and *The Order of Things*, Foucault shows that these knowledges have undergone transformations and reorganisations. He demonstrates the historicity of the concepts and objects with which these knowledges deal. He thus exposes the fragility of these concepts: far from a slow evolutionary refinement of concepts, there was more often a total incongruity between a concept developed at a particular period of cultural history and another concept developed later: 'a treatise of medicine written in 1780 and a treatise of pathological anatomy written in 1820', for example, 'belong to two different worlds' (1980a:211). Foucault went on to assert in retrospect that the field of positivity he postulated as the conditions of these knowledges implied an economy of power relations. This is most clearly stated in the opening chapter of *Discipline and Punish*:

> We should admit . . . that power produces knowledge (and not simply by encouraging it because it serves power or by applying it because it is useful); that power and knowledge directly imply one another; that there is no power relation without the correlative constitution of a field of knowledge, nor any knowledge that does not presuppose and constitute at the same time power relations. (1977a:27)

Pursuing this theme in a lecture from roughly the same period, Foucault went on to argue that

> in a society such as ours, but basically in any society, there are manifold relations of power which permeate, characterise and constitute the social body, and these relations of power cannot themselves be established, consolidated nor implemented without the production, accumulation, circulation and functioning of a discourse. There can be no possible exercise of power without a certain economy of discourses of truth which operates through and on the basis of this association. We are subjected to the production of truth through power and we cannot exercise power except through the production of truth. (1980a:93)

The very existence and development of the 'human sciences' constitutes a historical event peculiar to our society, and one that must be accounted for. Foucault's writings on the question of power are best approached as part of this endeavour. Ironically, as we hope to demonstrate, he is less concerned with 'power' as an entity or process than with an interrogation of contemporary western societies. In his words, 'I in no way construct a theory of power', rather:

> In many instances I have been led to address the question of power only to the extent that the political analysis of power which was offered did not seem to me to account for the finer, more detailed phenomena I wish to evoke when I pose the question of telling the truth about oneself. (1990:39)

His objective is therefore quite practical: to expose the *political and strategic nature* of those ensembles of knowledge previously thought to be either relatively independent of power (the 'human sciences'); or (as in the case of criminology or sexuality) linked only in a vague or inadequate way to political institutions.

Let us begin therefore by examining Foucault's conceptualisation of modern society. This will not only clarify his insistence on the need to retheorise the concept of power, but also make intelligible the methods of analysis he recommends in response.

An ontology of the present

In an essay in which he reflects on Kant's reflections on the Enlightenment, Foucault places himself in a philosophical tradition inaugurated by Kant and concerned with critically evaluating one's own historical epoch or 'present'. Foucault called this project 'an ontology of the present' (1986b:96), and distinguished it from other critical versions of philosophy as not being concerned with exposing the *general* conditions determining the production of all truth. An ontology of the present would instead aspire to unearth the particular *historical* conditions which produced the types of 'scientific' truths peculiar to our society. By using the term 'ontology', Foucault emphasises the metaphysical or interpretive nature of this enterprise: his assessment of the history of our 'present' is not intended as a definitive statement or unproblematic 'truth', but merely as one contribution to an ongoing debate about the nature of the world we find ourselves in.

To produce an ontology of the present involves detaching oneself from one's cultural surroundings. It poses a series of questions intended to undermine the familiarity of our 'present', to disturb the ease with which we think we know ourselves and others. Previously this critique had been conducted, most notably by Max Weber and the early Frankfurt School of social theorists, in terms of the question of what constitutes the defining characteristics of 'modernity'. Foucault thought that if our conceptions of power had hitherto been mistaken, and if power had been inadequately analysed or neglected within contemporary philosophy, this was because our basic conceptualisation of modern society (and, as a consequence, 'ourselves') had also been erroneous. The two cannot be separated: a new analysis of power requires shaking off accepted and familiar ways of conceiving of 'modernity'. At the same time, we can gain a more complex picture of modern western society by attending to the problem of power in greater depth.

Foucault provides a novel and somewhat surprising conceptualisation of our 'present', suggesting that a society's 'threshold of modernity' has been crossed when 'power' is primarily a matter of the administration of 'life' (1979a:143). This is a difficult point and we will need to come back to it, for it forms the cornerstone of Foucault's conception of modern society.

It would seem at first sight that *all* forms of government in all societies are primarily concerned with the problem of 'life'. In fact, it seems so obvious as almost to go without saying. But one way to illustrate Foucault's thesis is to make a comparison with ancient Greek society (Foucault, 1986a), where, for example, the various forms of political organisation were in no way charged with responsibility over the *biological* needs of the citizenry, and nor did they conceive of the population as a living species-body. By contrast, Foucault argues that the government of biological needs, in both its individual and composite forms, constitutes the defining feature of our society. Methods of power in their modern forms have assumed responsibility for life processes: births, deaths, sexual relations, sickness, disease, bodily hygiene, and so on. They have undertaken, as their principal form of government, the control and modification of these life processes.

> For the first time in history, no doubt, biological existence was reflected in political existence; the fact of living was no longer an inaccessible substrate that only emerged from time to time, amid the randomness of death and its finality; part of it passed into knowledge's control and power's sphere of intervention. Power would no longer be dealing simply with legal subjects over whom the ultimate domination was death, but with living beings, and the mastery it would be able to exercise over them would have to be applied at the level of life itself; it was the taking charge of life, more than the threat of death, that gave power its access even to the body. (1979a:143)

Political strategies within our society revolve around the question of 'life': the demands for basic needs, for the realisation of potentials, for the annihilation of scarcity and the concomitant demand for complete fulfilment and plenitude.

Foucault challenges two dominant conceptions of modernity by these claims. The first characterises our modern epoch primarily by the existence of a capitalist mode of production. The dominant struggle within our society, therefore, is a class struggle between the bourgeoisie and the working class. This forms the basis of Marxist analyses of modernity. The second, associated with the writings of Max Weber, opposes modernity to 'traditionalism' in terms of the evolution of reason. Scientific knowledges are the most exemplary instance of the maturity of reason. But concomitant with this development was its negative underside: instrumental rationality. Weber claimed that the evolution of a rational but depersonalised system of bureaucracy is the characteristic feature of modern society and one of the alienating by-products of the spread of 'enlightened' practices.

While Foucault is clearly indebted to both of these conceptions, he extends them in a crucial way. Above all, modern society for Foucault heralds the existence, unique to itself, of a new 'mechanism' of power. This 'mechanism' is a new way of consolidating power into ensembles concerned with the management and administration of 'life'. Neither equivalent to the 'state' nor reducible to the effects of other more primary processes, it is a mechanism which ensures the efficient functioning of power's control over life processes. Foucault argues that in medieval society power had been consolidated largely through the existence of a sovereign authority who exercised absolute control over his subjects, primarily through the threat or open display of violence. In the modern era, power is co-ordinated in an altogether different way:

> In the seventeenth and eighteenth centuries, we have the production of an important phenomenon, the emergence, or rather the invention, of a new mechanism of power possessed of highly specific procedural techniques, completely novel instruments, quite different apparatuses, and which is also, I believe, absolutely incompatible with the relations of sovereignty. (1980a:104)

Foucault makes a number of contrasts which help to clarify the differences between a mechanics of power based on sovereignty and the type of mechanism which gradually came to replace it:

> This new mechanism of power is more dependent upon bodies and what they do than upon the earth and its products. It is a mechanism of power which permits time and labour, rather than wealth and commodities, to be extracted from bodies. It is a type of power which is constantly exercised by means of surveillance rather than in a discontinuous manner by means of a system of levies or obligations distributed over time. It presupposes a tightly knit grid of material coercions rather than the physical existence of a sovereign. It is ultimately dependent upon the principle, which introduces a genuinely new economy of power, that one must be able simultaneously both to increase the subjected forces and to improve the force and efficacy of that which subjects them. (1980a:104)

By introducing the issue of power as a phenomenon to be differentiated historically, Foucault sets himself apart from all other contemporary social theorists. It is crucial to stress this point as it is often overlooked by commentators and leads to serious misunderstandings. McNay, for example, claims that Foucault's account of power lacks 'differentiation'; and that he fails 'to conceive of power in any other way than as a constraining form of corporeal control' (McNay, 1992:44). This criticism is the result of not grasping Foucault's emphasis on the *historical* specificity of whatever forms of power exist in any society. It is equivalent to accusing Marx of failing to differentiate systems of economic production. Foucault's point was that power in its modern form precisely does *not* act as a constraining form of 'corporeal control'. If it did, there would be no need to explain its operations. But, on the contrary, precisely what need to be explained are the methods whereby 'time and labour' can be 'extracted' from bodies, when those modern bodies are not necessarily physically constrained, possess legal rights preventing exploitation, and are 'free' from direct forms of control.

Indeed, McNay's observations would serve more adequately as a criticism of all *non*-Foucauldian conceptions of power—including the feminist conception held (but never made explicit) by McNay. Foucault claimed that all contemporary analyses of power are based on one or another version which portrays it as negative and repressive. They tend to identify power only in the form of a relationship between a sovereign and a subject (or subjects). Most commonly, this mode of analysis depicts the 'state' as the more recent equivalent of a sovereign, and posits free 'individuals' as the subjects under the state's control.

Foucault's writings on the topic of power are aimed primarily at this conception. Among other problems, to limit considerations of power to its sovereign conception seriously underestimates the diverse, even 'polymorphous', character of the relations of force extant in our society, and leaves unexplained the mechanisms required to connect and consolidate these relations. The most significant feature of Foucault's thesis is his stress on the *productive* nature of power's modern exercise. His main aim was to turn a negative conception upside down and attribute the production of concepts, ideas, and the structures of institutions to the circulation and exercise of power in its modern forms. He forcefully expresses this point in the following passage: 'We must cease once and for all to describe the effects of power in negative terms: it "excludes", it "represses", it "censors", it "abstracts", it "masks", it "conceals". In fact, power produces; it produces reality; it produces domains of objects and rituals of truth' (1977a:194).

But Foucault's emphasis on the historical specificity of our productive forms of power has a further important consequence: it distinguishes his mode of analysis from others—primarily structuralism—which also stress the 'productive' character of all facets of culture. Far from 'repressing' our inherent nature, argue such theorists as Lacan and Kristeva, cultural forces positively 'produce' what we come to view as intimate parts of ourselves: we can know ourselves only on the basis of what a cultural totality dictates. This leads some commentators to see very little difference between Foucault and structuralist enterprises. Forrester, for example, claims there is nothing original about Foucault's thesis on power because some versions of structuralist thought had already asserted the positivity and generative capacity of structures. Foucault merely substitutes 'power' where the structuralists had referred to a 'centre':

> The French structuralists' programme always emphasised the 'system', the network of linkages, the webs of relations . . . Shorn of its antithetical references to the weight of negative law, and to the absolute right of refusal of the sovereign, Foucault's espousal of a positive concept of power does not seem so strikingly novel. (Forrester, 1990:305)

But in response we could note, as did Foucault, the 'strangely restrictive way' this positive power is defined in structuralist formulations: 'poor in resources, sparing of its methods, monotonous in the tactics it utilizes, incapable of invention, and seemingly doomed always to repeat itself' (1979a:85). In other words, power cannot be theorised as 'positive' while it remains historically *undifferentiated.* Foucault differed from structuralist analysts by retrieving the concept of power from its vague identification with a general cultural totality. By doing so, he discovered that the economy of 'power', like the economy of production, has a history. We can now talk of systems of *power relations* rather than a general concept of 'power'. This played no small part in Foucault's ability to define with more complexity the cultural ensembles which comprise our modernity.

In short, Foucault suggests that power is intelligible in terms of the *techniques* through which it is exercised. Many different forms of power exist in our society: legal, administrative, economic, military, and so forth. What they have in common is a shared reliance on certain *techniques* or methods of application, and all draw some authority by referring to scientific 'truths'. Later, we will see that these techniques (the Panopticon and the confessional, for example), like any other form of applied knowledge, have a history—and this is what allows for the differentiation of systems of power relations. Foucault's point is to stress that there are no *necessary* or universal forms for the exercise of power to take place: our society bears witness to the production of quite specific practices which characterise the ways in which power relations function within it.

Because all of this remains a very general presentation of Foucault's retheorisation of power, we will now consider how Foucault conducted his analyses of power in two specific apparatuses (*dispositifs*): criminality and sexuality. Clearly, these were not chosen randomly as topics of investigation, for they cogently illustrate the history of the type of mechanisms of power he wishes to expose. In other words, in providing examples of the functioning of this type of power and the effects it produces, Foucault makes a political statement about the nature of our society. Whether or not we agree with this assessment, it is difficult to deny its relevance, force, and 'originality'.

A disciplined society

In contrast to any conception of the social body based on sovereignty, Foucault calls the mechanisms of power we have been discussing 'disciplinary power'. The central text here is *Discipline and Punish*, a book which deals ostensibly with the rise of the prison and the novel form of punishment of criminals that accompanied it. The primary difference between the two regimes of punishment, *pace* McNay, is that retribution for one's crimes was no longer enacted on the criminal's *body*. Criminality turned instead to adopt modern techniques of power. Thus one of Foucault's main arguments is that only a particular *mode of society* could have invented this form of punishment:

> Our society is one not of spectacle, but of surveillance; under the surface of images, one invests bodies in depth; behind the great abstraction of exchange, there continues the meticulous, concrete training of useful forces; the circuits of communication are the supports of an accumulation and a centralization of knowledge; the play of signs defines the anchorages of power; it is not that the beautiful totality of the individual is amputated, repressed, altered by our social order, it is rather that the individual is carefully fabricated within it, according to a whole technique of forces and bodies. (1977a:217)

The types of instruments and techniques used by the operations of disciplinary power can be taken over and used by *any* institution: penitentiaries, certainly, but also schools, hospitals, military centres, psychiatric institutions, administrative apparatuses, bureaucratic agencies, police forces, and so on. Modern criminology constitutes an 'apparatus' composed of power relations co-ordinated in relationships with systems of knowledge.

When considered from any point of view other than the history of power relations, Bentham's invention of the Panopticon represents a minor episode in the history of technologies, or perhaps of architecture. The design of the Panopticon consisted of a tower in the centre surrounded by a ring-shaped building composed of cells, each housing a prisoner. The Panopticon allowed for the continuous observation of inmates, while simultaneously requiring few supervisory resources. It enabled the old 'houses of security', with their chains, heavy locks and fortress-like structures, to be replaced by a well-arranged and much more economic unit. In the light of Foucault's work, this event was an important effect of disciplinary power and a significant contribution to the 'machinery' required for its functioning.

Panopticism is the exemplary technique through which disciplinary power is able to function. For it relies on 'surveillance' and the internal training this produces to incite states of docility; it need not rely on displays of physical force or violence. Direct force represents merely frustrated or failed forms of discipline. The subject of surveillance, by contrast, disciplines him- or her*self*:

> Hence the major effect of the Panopticon: to induce in the inmate a state of conscious and permanent visibility that assures the automatic functioning of power. So to arrange things that the surveillance is permanent in its effects, even if it is discontinuous in its actions; that the perfection of power should tend to render its actual exercise unnecessary; that this architectural apparatus should be a machine for creating and sustaining a power relation independent of the person who exercises it; in short, that the inmates should be caught up in a power situation of which they are themselves the bearers. (1977a:201)

The Panopticon is a machine designed to carry out procedures for the alteration of behaviour and to train or 'correct' individuals. The modern mode of punishment centres on the attempt to reform the criminal's 'soul'. This stands in stark contrast to the types of public executions routinely practised up to, and sometimes beyond, the eighteenth century. Foucault describes, at the beginning of the book, this earlier violent and deadly mode of punishment. It was performed directly on the criminal's body, as a 'display' of the awesome power of a sovereign authority, in retribution for a crime such as regicide. The shift towards imprisonment as a method of punishment is usually attributed to a general 'humanisation' which accompanied the transition to modernity.

For Foucault, however, it represents a stage in the 'normalisation' of individuals which is necessary for the government of life-processes. To investigate the dividing line between the 'normal' and the 'abnormal' is crucial in a social organisation dedicated to the administration of life. It finds a site of application in the study of criminals—their impulses, psycho-social make-up, and so forth. This form of study harnesses general knowledges about any individual: 'The individual and the knowledge that may be gained of him belong to this production' (1977a:194). Foucault points out that in a prison criminals are categorised not according to the crimes they commit but according to the 'dispositions' of the individual offender. 'The prison became a sort of permanent observatory that made it possible to distribute the varieties of vice or weaknesses' (1977a:126). The Panopticon furnishes the conditions necessary for these procedures and provides a masterly 'solution' to the problem of housing criminals in a designated and confined space.

The Panopticon was accompanied by, and found its support in, a variety of training techniques which Foucault calls 'disciplines'. Again, these 'disciplines' were by no means confined to the prison. Rather, they reflect a wider societal emphasis on *rational* procedures as the most effective way of inducing certain bodily effects. Foucault argues that the birth of the 'disciplines' inaugurated a certain 'art' of the human body. This art certainly aimed at extending the skills of the body, but it was more concerned with reorganising the body's forces so as to foster 'useful' obedience. 'What was then being formed was a policy of coercions that act on the body, a calculated manipulation of its elements, its gestures, its behaviour. The human body was entering a machinery of power that explores it, breaks it down and rearranges it' (1977a:138).

'Discipline' proceeds in four major ways. First, by the *spatial* distribution of individuals in certain ways. Most often this is done by enclosure. In the case of the prison, the criminal is separated from others in the community by being confined to a single place (the same is true of the psychiatric patient). But the distribution of space is also achieved by partitioning certain groups of individuals from others (students from workers); or by integrating individuals within machines of production housed in the same space, as in the architectural plan of a factory; or, again, by a network of relations of rank (officers separated from other ranks, as in a military barracks). By these procedures, one 'knows one's place' in the general economy of space associated with disciplinary power.

A second manifestation of discipline at work is the way the control of *activities* is brought into effect. One of the characteristics of disciplinary power is its tendency to extract 'time and labour' rather than 'wealth and commodities' from bodies. The control of activity is one of the primary ways by which 'time' can be 'extracted' from bodies: by the daily timetable; by adjusting movements such as marching to temporal stages; by correlating bodily positions and gestures, such as the 'gymnastics' associated with the mundane act of good handwriting; and by articulating the movements of the body with an object such as a rifle. Discipline is not guided by the principle of non-idleness or the imperative to not 'waste' time. Rather, it seeks 'to intensify the use of the slightest moment'; it is a matter of breaking down a set period of time into 'ever more available moments' (1977a:154). Moreover, discipline seeks to control the activities of bodies precisely because it recognises that the body is not 'mechanical'. Discipline conceives of the body as a 'natural' body, 'the bearer of forces and the seat of duration' (1977a:155). The body does not automatically align itself into a clockwork composition of actions: it has to be trained to do so. Thus we cannot say that discipline is guided by a 'false' or ideological conception of the human body. Rather, it actively seeks to cultivate a certain type of body on the basis of knowledge considered 'true'.

Thirdly, discipline also concerns the organisation of *segments or stages* of training. This is directly relevant to pedagogical practices. Disciplinary power develops a general code for the transition from student to master, put into practice in various fields of learning. It codifies segments in terms of a hierarchy, where each stage of the learning process is significantly more difficult than the last. This enables the development of skills to be carefully monitored while also providing a way to differentiate, or individualise, novices.

Finally, discipline also brings into effect a general *co-ordination* of all elementary parts. Such a combination requires that the training procedures directed at the human body are integrated into a more general 'machinery'; that chronological series also become pieces of the machinery; and that a precise system of commands is activated. In order to achieve this co-ordination, discipline relies on what Foucault calls 'tactics'. These ensure that 'the product of the various forces is increased by their calculated combination' (1977a:167). Critics often charge Foucault's conception of institutions with being excessively functional or anonymous and leaving no room for conscious agency. But this is not the case. For Foucault, an institution is composed of *opposing* forces likened only to a state of war. Disciplinary institutions thus require an ever-alert attention to the 'government' of all composite parts and the invention of certain tactical manoeuvres to ensure the implementation of disciplines. For Foucault, this is the essence of modern 'politics': inverting Clausewitz's assertion that 'war is politics continued by other means', he argues that '"politics" has been conceived as a continuation, if not exactly and directly of war, at least of the military model as a fundamental means of preventing civil disorder' (1977a:168). Elsewhere Foucault elaborates on this point in an important way, pointing out that tactics within institutions are often part of a more general political 'strategy'. Using the example of psychiatry he observes that

> in order for a certain relation of forces not only to maintain itself, but to accentuate, stabilise and broaden itself, a certain kind of manoeuvre is necessary. The psychiatrist had to manoeuvre in order to make himself recognised as part of the public hygiene system. (1980a:206)

By using the term 'discipline' to designate these training procedures, Foucault stresses also the connections between these techniques of power and the forms of knowledge that developed alongside them. As mentioned previously, knowledge gained on the basis of disciplinary power is formulated according to 'norms' of behaviour. But what is centrally at issue is the types of *instruments* and *procedures* that harness the accumulation of knowledge. They all involve some form of unequal intercourse between two agents or parties. In the case of observation, the traffic of surveillance travels only one way: towards the subject upon whom the technique is exercised. The subject of surveillance does not have the reciprocal power to 'observe' the observer. Likewise, in the case of those normalising judgements which determine an individual's level of 'deviancy', one person has the capacity to judge someone else on the basis of knowledge that only the former possesses. And in the case of examinations, it is only the subject of power who undergoes this trial; it is set by someone already possessing the skills or knowledge the other is seeking.

According to Foucault (1980a:105), disciplinary power was one of the great 'inventions' of bourgeois society and is the primary means whereby the 'cohesion' of this type of social body is ensured and maintained. But disciplinary power cannot thereby be seen simply to 'reflect' the requirements of the economic (capitalist) base. Foucault thus challenges those Marxist conceptions of modernity which claim that economic forces determine other social factors—at least 'in the last instance'. Foucault argued on a number of occasions that power is a much more 'material' force than the exigencies demanded by economic priorities. Disciplinary power played an indispensable role in the constitution of industrial capitalism, while simultaneously determining the characteristics of 'bourgeois' life.

Returning to Foucault's assessment that modern society ushered in the age of the government of 'life' and 'life-processes', we can see that the techniques associated with disciplinary power must exist at least logically prior to the employment of other technologies for other purposes—such as the accumulation of capital. In directing power at the level of life itself, one aims to optimise its forces and aptitudes in order to mould them towards certain goals and particular ends. Discipline produces 'practised' bodies; it 'increases the forces of the body (in economic terms of utility) and diminishes these same forces (in political terms of obedience)' (1977a:138). Capitalism would not have been possible without the controlled 'insertion' of bodies into the production processes. Men and women had first to be 'accumulated' via the types of techniques of power we have discussed. In any case, it is probably more useful not to separate the two phenomena:

> In fact, the two processes—the accumulation of men and the accumulation of capital—cannot be separated; it would not have been possible to solve the problem of the accumulation of men without the growth of an apparatus of production capable of both sustaining them and using them; conversely, the techniques that made the cumulative multiplicity of men useful accelerated the accumulation of capital. (1977a:221)

Similarly, the processes of normalisation associated with disciplinary power do not necessarily produce conformity or the monotonous regularity of identities often claimed in radical critiques. On the contrary, one of the prime effects of disciplinary power was to produce, precisely, individuality. This is one of the significant features of Foucault's thesis on power. We must not make the mistake of thinking that techniques of power have crushed those natural forces which mark us as distinct types of human beings with various 'personality' traits. Rather, differences, peculiarities, deviance and eccentricities are ever more highlighted in a system of controls concerned to seek them out. The very notion of a 'personality' *derives* from this process: 'as power becomes more anonymous and more functional', Foucault writes, 'those upon whom it is exercised tend to be more strongly individualized'. 'In a system of discipline, the child is more individualized than the adult, the patient more than the healthy man, the madman and the delinquent more than the normal and the non-delinquent' (1977a:193).

The intention may have been to produce regularity, but the *effect* was quite the opposite: a multiplicity of disparate and variegated identities. Individuality is a modern phenomenon—just as, conversely, the supposedly liberatory demand for the recognition of 'individuality' and 'difference' springs from the same source. Indeed, Foucault's stress on this ironic consequence is an important point and a central feature of his conception of subjectivity:

> The individual is not to be conceived as a sort of elementary nucleus, a primitive atom, a multiple and inert material on which power comes to fasten or against which it happens to strike, and in so doing subdues or crushes individuals. In fact, it is already one of the prime effects of power that certain bodies, certain gestures, certain discourses, certain desires, come to be identified and constituted as individuals. The individual, that is, is not the *vis-à-vis* of power; it is, I believe, one of its prime effects. (1980a:98)

On this basis, however, certain theorists have attributed to Foucault a general theory of 'embodied' individualism, or a general theory of the relationship between a body and 'power'. It is worthwhile challenging these readings, for they often contribute to a misunderstanding of Foucault's claims about 'resistance' to power. McNay (1992:46) attributes to Foucault's work on power a 'theory of the body'; a theory, moreover, which is lacking because of its inattention to 'the gendered character of the disciplined body'. Likewise, Diprose (1991:4) attributes to Foucault's studies of normalising techniques a concern with 'embodiment' as the site of one's 'ethos'. She goes on to say: 'The suggestion is that bodies are made, not given, and that they are made to fit properly within a certain social structure'. And in a similar vein, Braidotti (1991:89) asserts that 'Foucault displaces and expands the notion of materialism, by inscribing it in the corpor(e)ality of the subject'.

But to attribute to Foucault a 'theory' of embodiment is to reduce his thesis on power to its least interesting dimension. Moreover, it places his work within a tendency which has dominated philosophy since the nineteenth century but of which Foucault was explicitly critical: the 'anthropological sleep'. This tendency is governed by the question, 'What is man?' and dedicates itself to discovering the true finitude of 'man'—through a mixture of empirical and transcendental assumptions. Foucault is not asking the question, 'What is man?' or much less, 'What is woman?'—two questions which, notwithstanding the views of Spivak (1982:185–6), would have to be taken as two sides of the same enquiry. Instead, Foucault is asking these questions: What is our historical present? What are the institutions and systems of knowledge that critical theorists think they can readily identify? What are the relationships between them within particular ensembles which characterise our present epoch?

Thus Foucault's argument that disciplinary power produced a certain 'art' of the human body challenges conceptions of *modernity* and only indirectly concerns empirical conceptions of the 'body'. By neglecting changing techniques of power in their accounts of modernity, theorists of a wide variety of persuasions have overlooked the 'art' required to produce the modern individual. Foucault's exposure of the relationship between individuality and recent devices of power puts an end to the idea that labour-power, or any other bodily capacity, is a 'given' human attribute. But the purpose of this argument is not to expose the fact that bodies are 'made'—something we knew already—but to challenge the idea that modernity can be adequately conceived as a system of capitalism attended by its state apparatuses. If labour-power is not 'given', then one must account for its production. But this then gives rise to a far more complex picture of modern society than Marxism allowed—a conceptualisation that feminists, too, would have to contend with in their accounts of modern 'patriarchy'.

The failure to register adequately Foucault's problematic mars Bartky's attempt to make good Foucault's 'gender blindness'. She too sees Foucault as providing a general theory of the relationship between a body and power, and uses his conceptualisation of a 'disciplinary' society to study the production of 'docile' female bodies, the machinery 'that turns a female body into a feminine one' (1988:78). Bartky's prime concern is to explain why women torture their bodies in an effort to look 'beautiful'. She attributes this imperative to the 'disciplinary power' compelling women to inscribe their bodies with 'femininity'—power emanating from sources as varied as friends, doctors, 'beauty' experts, glossy magazines and images of women on film and television. While she rejects any simplistic notion of 'false consciousness' behind these actions, Bartky nevertheless asserts that a 'generalised male witness comes to structure woman's consciousness of herself as a bodily being' (1988:77). This is the result of dominant male 'norms' in society. Using Foucault's 'positive' conception of power, and opposing it to traditional and repressive forms of power based on authority, Bartky conceives of these norms as producing the types of female bodies needed by patriarchal society.

But Foucault's retheorisation of the concept of power cannot reveal to us how a 'female' body is turned into a 'feminine' one. Instead, by claiming that historical conditions positively produce forms of consciousness or subjectivity, what Foucault *can* account for is why female subjects today are *different* from those of the past: in Foucault's schema, one of the main reasons is that power techniques have changed. Even if we accept that forms of patriarchy have always demanded that women beautify themselves in order to please men (and even this may be too generalised), they presumably will not do so in the same ways and not for identical reasons. Bartky suggests as an aside, in fact, that in contemporary society women may be dressing up for other women: male 'norms' provide a subversive way of practising this, in spite of the lack of formal legitimation.

Foucault provides a way of situating, historically, forms of masculine and feminine consciousness. This includes of course a 'feminist' consciousness. When Bartky poses the question as to why all women are not feminists, she neglects to investigate the far more puzzling issue inherent in the converse: how come, historically, there are any feminists at all? Such a configuration of power suggested by the notion of a 'generalized male witness' structuring 'consciousness' would seem to preclude a feminist identity. In ancient Greek society as studied by Foucault (1986a:154), girls were commonly married off at fifteen to men twice their age. Unlike today, women were not at that time considered to possess desire. The sexual infidelity of wives was therefore not an issue—it did not even enter the realm of dominant male thought (1986a:163). This stands in stark contrast to the effects of Christian and (later) medical problematisations of women's sexuality.

In short, to historicise power in Foucault's terms and relate it to the production of certain types of bodies is to say something about the configuration of our historical conditions—a history that both male and female bodies are enmeshed within. It is to observe that the 'souls' of our modern configuration are conceived largely in terms of their bodily capacities. Again, as we have seen, *Discipline and Punish* was 'intended as a correlative history of the modern soul and of a new power to judge [it]' (1977a:23). But Foucault does *not* enter into the dispute about the 'nature' of embodiment in general. Whether bodies are 'really' this or that is strictly outside his problematic.

Nowhere perhaps is this 'productive' nature of modern techniques of power more forcefully stressed than in the first volume of *The History of Sexuality* (1979a). Let us now consider Foucault's analysis of the role of power in the domain he calls 'sexuality', and his views on the role of resistance or opposition to power.

Scientia sexualis

Foucault's analysis of the role of power in the production of sexuality tells us much more about the configuration of our present society than about the nature of 'sex'. But by linking contemporary sexual practices to our modern mechanics of power in the way he does, Foucault goes further than he had done previously in attempting to shift the terms of debates concerning 'identities' towards another domain: what we have chosen to call 'the ethical'. In the next chapter we show that Foucault entertains the possibility of a different 'economy of bodies and pleasures' and a different conception of subjectivity from that we have inherited, historically. He does this by contrasting our own practices with those of ancient Greece and Rome, and rethinking the relationship between subjectivity and desire as something that can be freed from the trammels associated with psychological or psychoanalytic accounts of 'sexuality'. Far from recommending the ancient systems as an alternative (which in any case would be impossible and quite contrary to the historical sensitivity present in all Foucault's work), he uses them as a way of opening up the exploration of other possibilities as such.

For Foucault, contemporary critical debate over the issue of sexuality is tied too firmly to the sovereignty conception of power he tried to abandon and replace. The introductory volume of his *History of Sexuality* clarifies his rejection of those conceptions of power which relate it to sexual practices only negatively in the form of repression:

> The question I would like to pose is not, Why are we repressed? but rather, Why do we say, with so much passion and so much resentment against our most recent past, against our present, and against ourselves, that we are repressed? By what spiral did we come to affirm that sex is negated? (1979a:8–9)

In Foucault's conception, 'sexuality' refers to a historically constructed apparatus: a dispersed system of morals, techniques of power, discourses and procedures designed to mould sexual practices towards certain strategic and political ends. Western erotic practices have a long history with many continuous features—perhaps the most significant being a repression or undervaluation of female pleasures. But Foucault's important point is that the conception of eroticism in terms of 'sexuality' is a modern and *bourgeois* phenomenon. Sexuality had its genesis in the bourgeois concern to 'maximise' life and promote the vigour, longevity and progeniture of its class. Sexuality was the affirmation of the life of this class. Just as the old ruling aristocracy distinguished itself in terms of its 'blood', so the bourgeoisie relies on symbolisation to stake its claim to distinctiveness. The difference is that, this time, the emphasis is on a healthy body and bountiful sexuality.

Sex and sexual practices assumed crucial importance as a political issue in a society concerned with the management and direction of life-processes. According to Foucault, this was because sex linked the two centres of regulation of life which disciplinary power took charge of: the physical body as a biological organism, and the population as a living species-body. 'The disciplines of the body and the regulations of the population constituted the two poles around which the organization of power over life was deployed' (1979a:139). Both are encompassed by the term 'bio-power'.

We have already examined the first of these series of regulations, centred on the techniques of training, and comprising the 'disciplines': the optimisation of the body's forces and capabilities, the fostering of both the body's usefulness and docility, and the integration of this body into machines of production. The second series, which developed later and somewhat as a response to the first, focused on the *population* as a species. It comprised a series of interventions and supervisory regulations concerned to govern aspects of life such as propagation, births, mortality, contraceptive practices, the general level of health in the community, life expectancy, longevity, the natural conditions which can cause unexpected modifications of these processes (such as environmental factors).

Thus sex was a prime concern for both facets of bio-power, and enabled the two series to overlap and reinforce each other in their operations. Knowledge of sex played a crucial role in co-ordinating the administration of life. On the one hand, sex was relevant to the harnessing and distribution of the forces of the body; on the other, it was crucially important to the management of the population and the attempt to mould it towards certain desired effects. It

> fitted in both categories at once, giving rise to infinitesimal surveillances, permanent controls, extremely meticulous orderings of space, indeterminate medical or psychological examinations, to an entire micro-power concerned with the body. But it gave rise as well to comprehensive measures, statistical assessments, and interventions aimed at the entire social body or at groups taken as a whole. Sex was a means of access both to the life of the body and the life of the species. It was employed as a standard for the disciplines and as a basis for regulations. This is why in the nineteenth century sexuality was sought out in the smallest details of individual existences; it was tracked down in behavior, pursued in dreams; it was suspected of underlying the least follies, it was traced back into the earliest years of childhood; it became the stamp of individuality—at the same time what enabled one to analyze the latter and what made it possible to master it. But one also sees it becoming the theme of political operations, economic interventions (through incitements to or curbs on procreation), and ideological campaigns for raising standards of morality and responsibility: it was put forward as the index of a society's strength, revealing of both its political energy and its biological vigor. (1979a:145–6)

We have already mentioned Foucault's unearthing of the significant role played by Bentham's Panopticon in the operations of disciplinary power. In a similar vein, the treatment Foucault provides of the history of another technology, the confessional, becomes important for his thesis concerning the relationship between sexuality and power. Outside of a consideration of power relations, the confessional would seem to occupy only marginal importance as a religious ritual—at least from the perspective of political considerations.

But Foucault argues that the confessional has played a role for many centuries of western civilisation as 'the general standard governing the production of the true discourse on sex' (1979a:63). Therefore when the confessional underwent a transformation and became localised in various secular institutions, Foucault views this development as a significant contribution to technologies directed at sex and sexual relations. It is the means by which any subject in society is incited to generate true discourses concerning their erotic practices. But unlike its employment within the penitential practices of medieval Christianity, its employment within modern secular institutions aims at discovering quite different sorts of knowledge about the subject:

> It was a time when the most singular pleasures were called upon to pronounce a discourse of truth concerning themselves, a discourse which had to model itself after that which spoke, not of sin and salvation, but of bodies and life-process—the discourse of science. (1979a:64)

As Lydon (1988:136–7) observes, the Catholic Church in contemporary rural Ireland often substitutes itself in place of women's 'self-help' clinics: women in the confessional 'could learn the truth of their reproductive systems from their bishops, themselves no doubt goaded into speech by the women's own murmurings in the confessional'.

The confessional now enjoys a position as the privileged means whereby individuals become imbricated in procedures of 'truth-telling' in those areas of the administration of life which are directed at sexual practices. Like the Panopticon, the confessional has become an essential technique in the functioning of bio-power. But it is also a much more 'versatile' technology, allowing for employment in those areas or institutions of society either divorced from, or existing only on the fringes of, the state apparatus (such as relations within the family):

> The confession has spread its effects far and wide. It plays a part in justice, medicine, education, family relationships, and love relations, in the most ordinary affairs of everyday life, and in the most solemn rites; one confesses one's crimes, one's sins, one's thoughts and desires, one's illnesses and troubles; one goes about telling, with the greatest precision, whatever is most difficult to tell. One confesses in public and in private, to one's parents, one's educators, one's doctor, to those one loves; one admits to oneself, in pleasure and in pain, things it would be impossible to tell to anyone else, the things people write books about . . . Western man has become a confessing animal. (1979a:59)

The confessional can take the form of interrogations, interviews, conversations, consultations, or even autobiographical narratives. But wherever it is employed, it is a ritual that always unfolds within a power relationship. Foucault points out that one confesses to a real or imaginary partner who represents not just the other party of a dialogue 'but the authority who requires the confession, prescribes and appreciates it, and intervenes in order to judge, punish, forgive, console, and reconcile' (1979a:62). The confessional is employed most readily within those institutions which bear on the knowledge of sexual practices: psychoanalysis, psychiatry, medicine and pedagogy. These sciences 'carefully assembled' and classified people's pleasures. The confessional allowed for the reconstruction and interpretation of acts and events and incited the development of various forms of commentary on them.

One of the main themes of Foucault's thesis on sexuality was the rejection of the repressive hypothesis—associated with the psychotherapy of Wilhelm Reich—which stated that modern capitalist societies ushered in an age of increased sexual repression. Instead Foucault argues that there has been a veritable explosion of discourses concerning sex during the same epoch. For Foucault, when techniques of normalisation were applied to the question of sex and sexual relations, this produced a multiplication and intensification of precisely the deviant forms of bodily 'sexualities' it intended to regulate:

> Nineteenth-century 'bourgeois' society—and it is undoubtedly still with us—was a society of blatant and fragmented per-

> version. And this was not by way of hypocrisy, for nothing was more manifest and more prolix, or more manifestly taken over by discourses and institutions . . . At issue . . . is the type of power it brought to bear on the body and on sex. In point of fact, this power had neither the form of the law, nor the effects of a taboo. On the contrary it acted by multiplication of singular sexualities. It did not set boundaries for sexuality; it extended the various forms of sexuality, pursuing them according to lines of indefinite penetration . . . Modern society is perverse, not in spite of its puritanism or as if from a backlash provoked by its hypocrisy; it is in actual fact, and directly, perverse. (1979a:47)

Reich had attempted to merge the insights of Freud with those of Marxist politics. He asserted that, because of capitalism's need for a steady and abundant supply of labour-power, it was fair to assume that the sexual pleasures and habits of the working class would need to be 'curtailed' and repressed by bourgeois ideologies. Thus they would be shifted, apparently, to the serious business of reproduction as a kind of 'economising' of energies. But Foucault argues that this was not the case. Techniques of sexuality were applied first and foremost by the bourgeoisie to *themselves*.

Foucault illustrates his argument by pointing out that, if one adheres to the repressive hypothesis, the young adult working-class man who possesses nothing more than the life-force of his body was the figure most likely to be targeted by sexual technologies. But instead, it was the bourgeois schoolboy, 'surrounded by domestic servants, tutors and governesses' (1979a:121) who came under the spotlight. The schoolboy came under surveillance because he was in danger of compromising, not just his physical strength, but also his 'intellectual capacity, his moral fiber, and the obligation to preserve a healthy line of descent for his family and his social class' if he indulged in any untoward variety of 'secret pleasures' (1979a:121). The 'pedagogization of children's sex' was one of several strategic unities that comprised bourgeois techniques for the normalisation of sexual practices.

Turning to another of these unities, Foucault makes a similar point concerning the medicalisation of women's sexuality. The first figure to be 'invested' by technologies of sex was the supposedly 'idle' bourgeois wife. We can appreciate the importance this figure assumed in the light of Foucault's thesis concerning power and the management of 'life'. This was both because her biological body required a special definition independently of the masculine body, and also because women's greater reproductive capacity (in comparison to the role of men) signalled their greater propensity to generate *illness*. Further still, women represented a hangover from the old systems of alliance, where they had always 'to appear as a value'. But, simultaneously, women were at the forefront of the new system of sexuality, 'assigned a new destiny charged with conjugal and parental obligations' (1979a:121).

Foucault claims that, for a long time, the working class resisted and refused to accept the 'garrulous' form of sexuality characterising the bourgeoisie. This is not to suppose, in an ideal fashion, that the working classes were not subjected to other, equally forceful, pressures concerning kinship and alliance. But it is to say that, when it comes to a consideration of 'sexuality' as an ensemble of technologies and moralities, the bourgeoisie 'tried it on themselves first' (1979a:122). Foucault also makes it clear, however, that bourgeois 'sexuality' was by no means an 'all-encompassing strategy' present in a homogeneous way at all levels of the social body: 'There was no unitary sexual politics' (1979a:122). This leads him to a very interesting assertion which problematises the claims of both psychoanalysis and sexology concerning the assumed universality of sexual forms and relations:

> We must return, therefore, to formulations that have long been disparaged; we must say that there is a bourgeois sexuality, and that there are class sexualities. Or rather, that sexuality is originally, historically bourgeois, and that, in its successive shifts and transpositions, it induces specific class effects. (1979a:127)

Again, this claim is intelligible only in terms of Foucault's retheorisation of the concept of power. That is, if one no longer conceives of power as negative and repressive, and instead views it as positive and productive, one then attributes to power the capacity to produce the cultural forms and social stratifications we have come to recognise as features of our society.

This is important also in relation to Foucault's shift towards the analysis of subjectivity in terms of ethics. It is in the introductory volume of the *History of Sexuality* that the problem of the relationship between power and subjectivity is placed on the drawing-board. Foucault's thesis concerning sexuality makes an original contribution to the age-old philosophical question of 'being': subjectivity is intimately and inextricably bound up with regimes of 'power-knowledge'. For Foucault, the production of scientific truths about all facets of 'life' and life-processes is no longer an abstract or formal problem: it directly concerns the way we live and the ways in which we understand or experience those processes. It is not enough to hope that a 'better' truth is on its way. But neither can we be content simply to abandon belief in these truths, for they concern our very material existence: our experience of pleasure, illness, pain, suffering, joy, and so on. We are, in a sense, compelled to take a position, to 'speak' our minds or voice our opinions. But this imperative is also what ensures the continued exercise of power through subjects:

> I would say that we are forced to produce the truth of power that our society demands, of which it has need, in order to function: we *must* speak the truth; we are constrained or condemned to confess or to discover the truth. Power never ceases its interrogation, its inquisition, its registration of truth: it institutionalises, professionalises and rewards its pursuit. In the last analysis, we must produce truth as we must produce wealth, indeed we must produce truth in order to produce wealth in the first place. (1980a:93)

By bringing the problem of the production of truth to the level of subjection—via its connections to modern forms of power—Foucault also undermines those conceptions of resistance to power which are entailed, often implicitly, by some other critical social theories. Importantly, Foucault's formulation complicates the politics associated with human 'identities'. He asserts that, as disciplinary power continually multiplied its centres and localities, it produced, in the process, unprecedented sites of resistance. But resistance, in Foucault's conception of it, cannot be simply a reaction to a pre-existing power. 'This', he writes, 'would be to misunderstand the strictly relational character of power relations' (1979a:95). Resistance, in fact, is never in a position of *exteriority* in relation to power. Rather, it is more like the opposite: states of power are continually engendered or incited on account of the potential counter-powers which coexist with them.

Many critical commentators find this conception of resistance unsatisfactory. Diamond and Quinby (1988:xiv), for example, claim that Foucault is 'premature' in giving precedence 'to a generative mode of power' when he characterises western societies as having moved from a 'symbolics of blood' to an 'analytics of sexuality'. They assert that the type of power associated with the 'sovereign's right of death'—namely, the right to seize bodies and time—is still alive and well in contemporary societies and remains largely in the hands of men. This is essentially the same argument presented by Bartky (1988:82) when, following the claims of Dews, she accuses Foucault of lacking a theory of the 'libidinal body' which exists prior to power: 'domination (and the discipline it requires) are never imposed without some cost'.

But the problem with these criticisms is that they fail to implicate the interests of the contemporary analyst or critic in the 'struggle' at issue. To understand this point fully, we must be clear about what Foucault means by a 'power relation'. Power is nothing more and nothing less than the multiplicity of force relations extant within the social body. Power's conditions of possibility actually consist of this moving substrate of force relations: the struggles, confrontations, contradictions, inequalities, transformations and integrations of these force relations. Thus we are 'positioned' within any struggle only as a consequence of the existence of a struggle for power. If we repeat Foucault's assertion that 'politics is war pursued by other means', we can clarify his insistence that both domination *and* resistance to it involve the invention of 'tactics' and the co-ordination of these various different tactics into coherent strategies.

This is perhaps the most important political consequence of Foucault's thesis on power: a strategic manoeuvre must be countered by an opposing manoeuvre; a set of tactics must be consciously invented in opposition to the setting in place of another; a different 'art' of the human body is what will oppose a historically given one, and so on. Foucault's conception of resistance operates strictly on the level of discursive 'cultivation'. He does not posit an essential or excessive realm divorced from our historical present which harbours a hidden 'potential'. For such a realm is defined, paradoxically, by the very incapacity to define it or practise it under present, less than adequate, historical conditions. Importantly, this means that power relations are the bottom line, so to speak. It is not possible to slip natural 'bodies', or an internal voice, or a hidden soul underneath these relations:

> Relations of power are not in a position of exteriority with respect to other types of relationships (economic processes, knowledge relationships, sexual relations), but are immanent in the latter; they are the immediate effects of the divisions, inequalities, and disequilibriums which occur in the latter, and conversely they are the internal conditions of these differentiations; relations of power are not in superstructural positions, with merely a role of prohibition or accompaniment; they have a directly productive role, wherever they come into effect. (1979a:94)

Foucault admits, in a discussion of his methodology, that the connections between general political strategies and the particular historical investigations he undertakes (which he calls 'genealogies') are not tightly formulated and remain tentative (1981:4). In particular, the issue of the 'stability' and durability of bourgeois domination is perhaps not addressed adequately in his studies. The same could be said of the continuity of male domination in society. But this has more to do with his views about the role of intellectuals in modern society than with the shortcomings of his methodology. Foucault is more comfortable with interventions within specific problems or struggles than with general and overarching solutions to political questions. Indeed, Foucault views the latter as symptomatic of the inadequacies of radical critiques. Instead, he thinks of his genealogical researches as opening up 'spaces' for debate; they are 'propositions' or 'game openings' and are not meant as dogmatic assertions. At most, he says, 'they are philosophical fragments put to work in a historical field of problems' (1981:4).

Foucault is also clear that, although great radical ruptures or revolutions *have* taken place, and although rigid general divisions (usually in a binary form) do exist, what is much more important are 'mobile and transitory points of resistance' which are constantly shifting the focus with which these social cleavages are understood. It is the mundane or everyday acts of resistance that potentially produce profound effects.

Foucault claimed that one of the six identifiable characteristics of modern forms of struggle—against the types of power techniques that exist within our society—is that they are 'immediate' critiques of the instances of power closest to them. They are forms of opposition to the power of men over women, of parents over children, of psychiatrists over the mentally ill, of doctors over patients, of bureaucrats over citizens. The protagonist in these struggles does not hope to find solutions at a vague future date, but looks instead at the here-and-now and the immediate effects of the play of forces. Likewise, just as the state institutions have the capacity to harness and integrate micro-forces of power into general strategies, it is the 'strategic codification' of points of common resistance that makes radical change possible. These points of resistance, that is, traverse social stratifications or institutional unities: they cannot be 'pinned down' to a single set of positions or objectives. This point has been taken up by a feminist commentator:

> Depending upon where one is and in what role (eg. mother, lover, teacher, anti-racist, anti-sexist) one's allegiances and interests will shift. There are no privileged or fundamental coalitions in history, but rather a series of unstable and shifting ones. (Sawicki, 1986:30; see also Sawicki, 1991)

For Foucault, resistance is more effective when it is directed at a 'technique' of power rather than at 'power' in general. It is techniques which allow for the exercise of power and the production of knowledge; resistance consists of 'refusing' these techniques. But the unearthing of power techniques in their modern configurations requires conceiving of the social body as a multiplicity of force relations. Foucault suggests that power is intelligible, and susceptible to analysis down to its smallest details, in terms of the historical strategies and sets of tactics designed to mobilise these techniques to political advantage. But, importantly, oppressive forces of domination do not hold the monopoly in the capacity to invent tactics. If resistance is to be effective, it requires the active interrogation of the tactics employed in a struggle. But this means that one must acknowledge in the first place that tactics *are* being used. In other words, the ethical relationship of the protagonist to the 'power' being opposed and the historical position of this relationship must be made explicit.

Analysis

Foucault's 'ontology of the present' involves two interrelated dimensions: a challenge to accepted ways of conceiving of 'modernity' and a reassessment of the methods whereby the analysis of power had been previously conducted. We have tried to illustrate the particular method Foucault employs in his analyses of power and attempted to contrast his methodology with those of other critical theorists. Let us now examine this approach more systematically.

Foucault (1980a:115) claimed that analyses of power had been neglected within philosophical discourses because of a certain 'political situation' in Europe in the 1950s and 1960s. Power had been conceived in either one of two ways and remained unproblematised. The first consisted of equating power with the law and conceiving its exercise in juridical terms of constitution and sovereignty: sovereign rule exists as a result of a contract between two consenting parties or agents. By and large, this type of analysis was common among theorists on the conservative side of politics and derived its inspiration from early forms of political theory (such as Hobbes's theory of the state). Alternatively, power was analysed on the left side of politics, largely inspired by Marx, in terms of the state apparatus and its ideological 'representations' of power—as if power operated through deferred, discursive mechanisms. Both sides remained content to 'denounce' power as the global property of the 'other side'.

Yet, despite surface differences, both the 'juridical' and 'discursive' forms of analysis share a fundamental similarity, namely that power acts on something already constituted: that both the 'sovereign' who wields power and the 'subject' upon whom the power acts exist in this relationship *prior to* the exercise of power; that power is the *result* rather than the productive *cause* of this relationship. Both types of analyses tend to merge all forms of power relations into the terms of the general relationship of sovereign and subject. Foucault reinforced this point by assimilating the two forms of analysis into one and calling it the 'juridico-discursive' conception of power. He caricatured it by identifying the 'uniformity' of power's exercise within such a conception:

> Whether one attributes to it the form of the prince who formulates rights, of the father who forbids, of the censor who enforces silence, or of the master who states the law, in any case one schematizes power in a juridical form, and one defines its effects as obedience. Confronted by a power that is law, the subject who is constituted as subject—who is 'subjected'—is he who obeys. To the formal homogeneity of power in these various instances corresponds the general form of submission in the one who is constrained by it—whether the individual in question is the subject opposite the monarch, the citizen opposite the state, the child opposite the parent, or the disciple opposite the master. A legislative power on one side, and an obedient subject on the other. (1979a:85)

In the second of two lectures originally delivered in 1976, Foucault outlined five 'methodological precautions' to be borne in mind to avoid conceiving power in juridico-discursive terms of sovereignty (1980a:92–108). By way of summarising the content of this chapter, we will consider each point in detail.

First, Foucault stresses the *local and regional* points of power's destination as the focus of analysis, rather than a concentration on its 'central' and resultant forms. One should avoid the temptation of identifying global institutions, such as 'the state', as central conductors which orchestrate the movements of power. Instead, Foucault recommends investigation of those areas of relative autonomy: organisations which function daily in terms of their own procedures and techniques, in order to bring to light the *particular* configuration of power relations they depend on. In many such cases, these 'capillary' points of power's exercise surmount the influence and direction of state controls—yet their effects, of course, are no less significant for this.

Secondly, Foucault advocates the study of the '*effective* practices' of power, such as the Panopticon and the confessional. By turning attention to these technologies and their histories, Foucault avoids the tedious psychologism inherent in attempts to explain power in terms of intentions, motives, aims, interests or obsessions: the 'mind' of someone exercising power. For Foucault, what is important is the *effects* of power's exercise and not the myriad rationalisations offered to 'explain' why its actions take place. He refrains from providing a 'theory' about what power essentially 'is'. In addition, by attending instead to the practices and methods of power's exercise, he avoids attributing the devices of power to an 'author', either singular or collective.

The third methodological precaution relates to the tendency to view Power—with a capital 'P'—as the *homogeneous* domination over others by an individual or a group. This is an important point, for it is here that Foucault's displacement of a juridico-discursive conception of power is most apparent:

> Power must be analysed as something which circulates, or rather as something which only functions in the form of a chain. It is never localised here or there, never in anybody's hands, never appropriated as a commodity or piece of wealth. Power is employed and exercised through a net-like organisation. And not only do individuals circulate between its threads; they are always in the position of simultaneously undergoing and exercising this power. In other words, individuals are the vehicles of power, not its points of application. (1980a:98)

Likewise, Foucault's fourth recommendation overturns the related tendency to assume that power is exercised in a *descending* direction—from the lofty heights of the powerful down to the lowly depths of the powerless. Relevant here is the tendency to attribute the phenomenon of disciplinary power to the domination of the bourgeois class. Foucault states that class domination alone does not constitute an effective heuristic, for 'anything can be deduced from the general phenomenon of the domination of the bourgeois class' (1980a:100). The same could be said of feminist notions of 'patriarchy' and male domination. Instead, Foucault claims that one needs to investigate historically, and beginning from the lowest level of society, 'how mechanisms of power have been able to function' (1980a:100).

As such, Foucault recommends an *ascending* rather than descending analysis of power. Hegemonic or global forms of power rely in the first instance on those 'infinitesimal' practices, composed of their own particular techniques and tactics, which exist in those institutions on the fringes or at the micro-level of society (within the family, the classroom, and so on). What Foucault places at issue is how these mechanisms of power have been 'invested, colonised, utilised, involuted, transformed, displaced, extended' (1980a:99) by more general forms, leading to those types of social domination we can all readily identify.

Finally, Foucault stresses that the types of apparatuses of knowledge associated with the exercise of power cannot be considered systems of 'ideology'. Elsewhere, he argues, 'discourses are not once and for all subservient to power or raised up against it, any more than silences are' (1979a:101). While ideological productions certainly exist, they are much less important than the instruments and procedures which produce them, and what may be called the historical 'conditions' of this knowledge. What is important for Foucault about the technology of the confessional, for instance, is that it is employed in the first place: it reveals something about the nature of institutions in our society. The knowledge that springs from this technology may or may not be 'true'. The important point is that the technology is *effective* in producing what is considered as truth.

Foucault's retheorisation of power cannot be separated, therefore, from his analysis of the history of knowledges and technologies: the 'present' we find ourselves in. But it also complicates the politics associated with human identities, in so far as subjection involves an ethical dimension neglected by radical critiques. This is the focus of our final chapter.

4

The Subject

In his earlier work on historical transformation, Foucault refused to give priority to *individual creative* subjects. He was much more interested at that time in how particular kinds of subject (the mad, the ill, the criminal, the sexual pervert, for example) were *produced* as effects of discursive and power relations. That is, unlike many philosophers, Foucault refused to begin his investigation by taking for granted the idea of an autonomous and sovereign subject. Instead, his enquiries routinely turned to the historical conditions which made various types of quite specific and differentiated subjects *possible* in the first place.

But for all of this, Foucault never argued on behalf of the radical structuralist idea that there are no subjects, that the subject can be 'deleted' (Althusser, 1976:94–9) from philosophical thinking, even though his remarks in the final pages of *The Order of Things* on the disappearance of 'man' are sometimes read in this unfortunate way. Even at his most overtly political moment (in the traditional sense of 'political'), Foucault argues in *Discipline and Punish* against the idea that 'the soul is an illusion, or an ideological effect'. 'On the contrary', he continues, 'it exists, it has a reality, it is produced permanently around, on, within the body by the functioning of a power' (1977a:29). In the first volume of *The History of Sexuality* he analyses in greater detail how these processes of subject-production, or subjection, are effected by modern scientific forms of knowledge:

> The project of a science of the subject has gravitated, in ever narrowing circles, around the question of sex. Causality in the subject, the unconscious of the subject, the truth of the subject in the other who knows, the knowledge he holds unbeknown to him, all this found an opportunity to deploy itself in the discourse of sex. (1979a:70)

This relatively privileged scientific knowledge about both the exterior and the interior (body and mind) of the subject, however, was always only one side of the coin for Foucault. What Dreyfus and Rabinow call Foucault's 'genealogy of the modern individual as *object*' (1982:143–67) was never quite without its counterpart: the knowledge which the subject has of himself or herself. Indeed, particularly in the case studies of Rivière (1978a) and Barbin (1980b), Foucault's main focus was on the counter-discourses mobilised by these persons *against* the various dominant scientific accounts of their 'crimes' and 'transgressions'.

Let us remember, too, that the historical studies we have examined have all been directed not at history 'for its own sake' but at history in the service of understanding 'the modern soul'. Then we can begin to see the double strategy behind Foucault's second and third volumes of *The History of Sexuality* (1986a, 1988). First, by turning to ancient Greece and Rome, Foucault was able to explore a sexual ethics so extensively different from our own as to throw into vast relief the *specificity and peculiarity* of a government of the (sexual) subject by 'external' legal and scientific techniques. Secondly, by virtue of the fact that, particularly in ancient Greece, these 'external' techniques were *almost non-existent*, Foucault was able to explore a new topic which at the same time was relatively continuous with his previous work on subjection. This was an *ethical* enquiry centred not so much on the control of the subject by the external 'other' as on the internal relation of the self *to the self vis-à-vis* the question of proper sexual comportment. But for all this, it is manifestly an investigation of forms of *control.*

The sexual subject in ancient Greece

What is most immediately apparent to modern readers who turn to the medico-philosophical discussions of the fourth century BC is the relative absence of official (legal, moral, juridical) controls on sexual behaviour. It was not that laws did not exist: for example there was an absolute interdiction on extramarital relations for married women. Rather, sexual conduct appears to have been regulated in a totally different way and in relation to a different sphere of life. The mode of addressing problems was ethical (rather than simply legal) and the sphere of activity was the everyday care of the self. This sphere is best represented by the term 'ascetics' (from *askesis*, exercise, training or testing). One conducted oneself 'properly' in sexual matters neither because the law enjoined one to do so, on pain of punishment, nor because of ideas about deep-seated conceptions of evil (which would no doubt bring its own punishment in another life). Since the point of philosophy was not abstract thought alone, but thought in the service of good living, good sexual conduct was a question of the rather loose principles of training oneself. As today, austerity and abstention played their part, but in the name of an ascetics, an internal and external discipline, rather than ultimate public accountability.

This ethical surface consisted of four main regions:

- *health* (sexuality in relation to bodily functioning) and its associated disciplines of medicine and dietetics
- *the household* (sexuality in relation to those at home, the wife, the children, the slaves) and its associated discipline of economics
- *courtship* (sexuality in relation to boys) and its associated discipline of erotics
- *truth* (sexuality as a source of wisdom) and its associated discipline of philosophy.

Foucault begins his analysis of these four regions by offering what look like close continuities between them and our present regimes of health, marriage, 'homosexuality' and sexual truth.

Some ancient Greek texts warned of the *health* problems associated with 'seminal loss'. They considered it to be a disease, known as gonorrhea, which was 'shameful in itself' and 'dangerous in that it leads to stagnation; harmful to society in that it goes against the propagation of the species; and because it is in all respects the source of countless ills, it requires prompt treatment' (1986a:16). The discourses on *marriage* likewise held conjugal fidelity to be one of the highest virtues. Men could boast of their fidelity to their wives and be sure of a warm public reception. While not required by law, it was a sign of the man's 'inner strength, and self-mastery' (1986a:17). With respect to sexual relations between men and *boys*, while it is generally well known to have been condoned by the ancient Greeks, it is perhaps less well known that they routinely condemned it in cases where it led one of the partners (particularly the younger) towards 'effeminacy'. And lastly, turning now to more strictly *philosophical* matters, then as now, abstention and austerity were regarded as proper ways of conducting oneself. There was a massive interest in, if not cult of, chastity. For some, this was merely a matter of self-restraint which again attested to their high status; for others, chastity was a source of wisdom and access to the truth.

All of these forms are familiar to us today, if only as memories or hangovers from the fairly recent past: interdictions on masturbation for the sake of health; a pressure to conjugal fidelity; an association between pederasty and effeminacy; and the veneration of chastity as both strong-mindedness and as a discipline which can bring insights unavailable to others. But the mistake here is to assume that because those ancient Greek virtues and interdictions are superficially similar to their modern counterparts they are therefore *identical* with them and that a straightforward continuity exists between pagan and Christian practices and abstentions. It is certainly the case that many of the early church fathers cited the pagan works in support of the naturalness and eternal truthfulness of these proper ways. But they may have been less than happy to put each into its proper context. For when Foucault begins to inspect these four themes (the body, marriage, male–male relations and access to wisdom), he finds that the ethical complex of which they form the parts varies from period to period.

The ethical practices of Greek society in the fourth century BC differ (albeit in intensity and with minor modifications) from those of the first two centuries AD, and these in turn differ from medieval Christianity. To trace this development, we shall first look at Foucault's general picture of ancient Greek ethics. We shall then return to the four central themes (health, household, boys and truth). But instead of dealing with the early pagan and pre-

Christian (or 'imperial') periods separately (as Foucault does, one period per volume), we shall look at each field comparatively in the period from the fourth century BC to the second century AD.

Foucault's general characterisation of ethics in ancient Greece begins by noting its uniqueness in summoning 'the individual . . . to recognize himself as an ethical subject of sexual conduct' (1986a:32). It has its own style and flavour, and fits with a general view of the human subject which is utterly distinct from ours today. According to Foucault, any ethics, that is, any *ethos* of the self's relation to itself, has four components:

- an ethical *substance* (the ethical field as a whole, its *ontology* or theory of being)
- a type of *subjection* (the kinds of practices by which subjects formed and existed, its *deontology* or theory of duty)
- a typical *attitude* required of oneself (its *ascetics* or theory of training)
- a goal or *fulfilment* (its *teleology*, or theory of ends and purposes).

The ethics that concerns us here had unique and particular ways of meeting each of these requirements. Its ethical substance (ontology) was centred on the *aphrodisia*, a term we can translate as 'sexual pleasures'. But it also encompassed a range of practices we would rarely include in that category, and omitted a number of others we would think important. The pagan type of subjection (deontology) was formed around the concept of *chresis* or 'use', 'deployment'. The proper attitude (ascetics) to oneself was one of *enkrateia* or mastery. And the ethical goal was *sophrosyne* or moderation. What this amounted to was neither a rigid moral code like that of the early Christian period nor a set of laws for state intervention into the proper conduct of pleasure. Rather it consisted of a set of loose and general recommendations which 'stylised' (1986a:93) the proper use of one's pleasures. This was a period when ethics was more a matter of stylistics than of boundaries and interdictions. Ethics was an art.

Turning first to the *aphrodisia*, we could almost say that there was no 'sexuality' in ancient Greece (1986a:35), if by that we mean a single unitary concept. The term *aphrodisia* is plural and does not correspond to the Christian idea of the 'pleasures of the flesh'—either in its overtones of sinfulness or in its notion of a single phenomenon with, as it were, mere variations (homo-, hetero-, bi-, trans-, and the rest). Our idea of *sexuality*, by contrast with the Greek *aphrodisia*, 'does not just cover a wider area; it applies to a reality of another type' (1986a:35). To begin with, as the name suggests, these pleasures were loosely collected as 'the works, the acts of Aphrodite' (1986a:38). And this looseness appeared entirely suitable in ancient times. One did not want to be too precise. Not because of modesty for its own sake, but because precision itself was not appropriate in a sphere where each must make quite personal choices. This, then, is completely different from the 'long lists of possible acts', the tables that 'served to define what was licit, permitted, or normal' (1986a:38), that we now associate with the strong moral codes of the nineteenth century. Surprisingly, then, the supposedly sexually liberal ancient Greeks were quite reserved in their thinking about sex, and this reticence was simply an integral part of their thinking about pleasure.

However, this reticence, which can sound so similar to Christian prudery, was markedly different from it. It contained no element of suspicion (1986a:41). Instead, it was merely a kind of moderation and self-control—to be valorised, at its peak in men of great ethical strength and knowledge, but not to be punished if not exhibited. In addition, it is difficult to find in the literature anything vaguely resembling a catalogue of sexual *acts* (let alone of allowable versus illicit acts). This appears to be connected with a reduced interest in sexual forms, and its displacement by interest in the kinds of interior activities (desires) connected with them. If we therefore think of all possible sexual ethics as a triple arrangement of acts, desires and pleasures, we can contrast the Christian interest in the primacy of the act (and its type) with the earlier model, which attempted to integrate each element so that 'act, desire, and pleasure formed an ensemble whose elements were distinguishable certainly, but closely bound to one another' (1986a: 42). None of the elements appears to have been valorised separately at this time. Rather there was a circular arrangement in which desire provoked the sexual act, providing pleasure which, in turn, motivated desire. The Greek *aphrodisia*, above all, differed from our 'pleasures of the flesh' in that they were formed around this *dynamic* 'texture' (1986a:43).

One important 'variable' of this dynamic conception of sexuality was that it condoned and condemned the pleasures taken, not on the basis of the types of sexual act involved, but with regard to their *quantity*. Even when Plato speaks against relations between members of the same sex and on behalf of those between different sexes, it is not a speech for 'normality' and against 'abnormality'. If the pederastic pleasures are 'against nature', this is because they can lead to excess, according to Plato—to lack of moderation and 'self-restraint with regard to pleasure' (1986a:45). The condemnation does not arise (as it does so often today) from revulsion at the *act* and therefore the 'person'. It arises from the belief that 'the only offenses that one can commit are quantitative in nature' (1986a:45).

A second 'variable' around which the ancient Greeks defined sexual pleasure had to do with conceptions of active and passive roles. Great value was placed on agency: a man showed his virtue and virility by taking up the active position in intercourse, whether with a boy *or* a woman. Passivity was clearly associated with women and effeminate men; but this had less to do with moral acceptances and indictments than with the role one took in the little drama of sexual pleasure. And since its ethical injunctions were aimed purely at free men, we can begin to see that pagan philosophy had a very loose structure of *dos* and *don'ts*. They amounted to this: 'For a man, excess and passivity were the two main forms of immorality in the practice of the *aphrodisia*' (1986a:47).

If this was the limit of morality, then there was clearly no strong association between sexual pleasure and intrinsic evil. What we might now call 'guilt' was a potential that could arise only from too much pleasure or from pleasure gained in the passive role. The *aphrodisia*, by and large, were considered deeply natural, a part of being human. Nevertheless, they could be taxonomised further such that, for some philosophers, the specifically *sexual* pleasures were considered inferior to most others. And here lies a paradox that was solved in quite different ways at different times. For, if sexual pleasure is a natural human capacity, it is also one which human beings share with the animals. Unlike the higher pleasures, it has to do with bestial needs, basic instincts and the materiality of the body. Its 'naturalness', therefore, led to its association not only with goodness but also with the animal side of humanity. And because of the sheer intensity of sexual pleasure, by comparison with the other bodily pleasures of eating and drinking, built into it was a 'tendency to exaggeration, to excess' (1986a:49).

Platonic philosophy therefore wanted reason to triumph over a passion which could naturally and easily be overdone. And this was the basis for the mild prohibitions on excess. Foucault stresses that, despite some surface similarities, the Platonic counselling against sexual indulgence was utterly different from later Christian proscriptions of 'lust'. The latter emanates from ideas about the Fall from grace; while for Plato, over-indulgence was problematic because of the natural propensity for sexuality to tend to excess. This stemmed from a natural and abstract force, an *energia* (1986a:50), and the ethical question of how best to control and *use* this force. Nature's *energia* was thought to play itself out through the bodies and souls of men, not simply in the form of sexual 'urges' but also through the desires for food and drink. These three formed a grouping of 'common pleasures' or appetites in general. While separate, they 'constituted analogous ethical material' (1986a:51). And, for this reason, it is very difficult to separate the doctrines on eating and drinking from those on sexuality. Each deals with a common force and its proper *use*.

The second category, the 'type of subjection' to be found in ancient Greek ethics, is completely bound up with this problem of use (*chresis*). But 'use' was not simply a matter of utility; it had more to do with the 'stylistics' of sexual conduct. In fact the title, *The Use of Pleasure*, is a direct translation of the common Greek phrase, *chresis aphrodision* (1986a:53). Use and pleasure were intimately bound together in the form of an ethics of style; a style of managing nature's forces while simultaneously answering its calls. Again, it is very tempting to read Plato's and Xenophon's ideas about the proper forms of this regulation as a strict moral code. But in fact their directions had a totally different character, consisting more of strategies of proper exercise than of coded elements. Foucault looks at the three central strategies that constituted the proper use of pleasure.

The first of these is the 'strategy of need' (1986a:54–7). Here Foucault begins with the story of Diogenes, who was renowned not only for eating in the market place but also for relieving his sexual urges there. Diogenes' point of view on this was: why not? One has basic needs and requirements and nature has provided us with the means of their fulfilment. In fact, public masturbation, for Diogenes, was the simpler of the two fulfilments: 'Would to heaven that it were enough to rub one's stomach in order to allay one's hunger' (1986a:55). Unlike today's public masturbators, Diogenes' manual arts were not taken as signs of abnormality: he was simply seen to be working out a common doctrine centred on needs. The proper satisfaction of need meant its fulfilment to the minimum amount required by nature, and no more. Xenophon's Socrates counsels people to 'limit themselves to such indulgence as the soul would reject unless the need of the body were pressing, and such as would do no harm when the need was there' (1986a:55). The loose rule of need, therefore, depended on each examining his own, and finding its satisfaction exactly to that degree. This was nothing like a 'repression' of desires. Excess meant going beyond one's clearly felt needs: inducing artificial desires for food, drink or sex where none really existed in the soul. In this strategy, as in the others, therefore, we find not a moral prescription but advice on the beneficial arts of living; not self-control because of its offer of spiritual salvation but self-control as a means of *enhancing* one's pleasures.

The second strategy is that of 'timeliness' (1986a:57–9). It was often taken together with notions of the proper quantity (of food, drink, sex). Hence Plato says good fortune comes to those who take their pleasure 'at the right time and in the right amount' (1986a:57) and bad fortune to those who do not. Moreover, this general idea of 'the right time' straddled a whole range of ancient

Greek arts and sciences, from medicine to government and navigation. When to take a particular herb, when to exact a political measure, when to turn the ship to windward: these were related matters which connected the idea of self-control to the control of others. Accordingly, there was a proper period in one's life for sexual relations which would be injurious if practised when too young or too old. There was a time of each year, too, when sexuality was most beneficial. Then, further, there was the daily (or more strictly, nightly) timing of sexual conduct. Thus when Socrates speaks against incest, it is not only on behalf of a 'universal dictum, laid down by the gods' (1986a:59). In addition, punishment comes in the form of offspring who will 'come to no good' because their parents 'failed to respect the principle of the right time' (1986a:59). The immorality arises not simply from a contravention of divine law, but also from the parents 'mixing their seed unseasonably' (1986a:59).

The third and last strategy of the proper use of pleasure concerns the question of 'status'. According to this idea, it was proper to adjust one's conduct according to the social standing of one's sexual partner. This meant that the lower one's social status, the more expectable and tolerable were 'dishonourable' practices; and conversely, the higher one's rank, the greater the modesty and moderation expected. If one has 'attained distinction' then 'even a bit of negligence in some matter of high honor brings disgrace' (1986a:60). The disgrace, in this case, is a sign of weakness and a concomitant unfitness to rule. So, by extension, proper rulers were those who had the best aesthetics of living: government was tied to style of conduct. Hence a connection was formed between self-control in sexual conduct and the avoidance of political tyranny. It is in this way that the notion of 'the moderate state' (1986a:62) applied equally to civics *and* ethics. But the source of this (if any) was ethics rather than an imposition of morality by legislation. What, then, was this 'attitude' one was supposed to have to oneself?

It was no more or less than the third property of ancient ethics, the attitude of mastery or *enkrateia*. This is important for Foucault because there is a tradition of religious history which assumes

Christianity to involve a 'turning inwards' to oneself by contrast with a pre-Christian orientation to the outside world. Foucault suggests that this misses two essential phenomena: the aspect of Christian 'interiority', governed by a relation to oneself and based on clearly external moral codes; and the aspect of pagan life which was unquestionably focused on the attitude to the self, centred on *enkrateia*. This concept meant more than simply self-control. It was a term 'located on the axis of struggle, resistance, and combat' (1986a:65). Here the individual was compared with a city and its combative readiness. The city must be ready, kept alert, lest it is overcome. Mastery is, above all, an ethical *effort*.

Its first requirement is the effort involved in putting oneself into combat. The man who has never trained for fighting will never survive a real battle when it comes. Therefore we should not hope that our immodest desires will simply go away, but make ready for their eventual attack. We should acknowledge the strategy of our invading desires so that, in the hour of need, we will have the strength to overcome them and avoid becoming their slaves. Hence ethical conduct 'in matters of pleasure was contingent on a battle for power' (1986a:66), which meant actually putting oneself *in the way of* base feelings as a kind of practice for their defeat.

The second requirement of *enkrateia* was that the combat be fought within oneself. The invading desires were not thought of as merely external. On the contrary, they were part and parcel of oneself. One part of the self (the nobler part) was expected to combat and defeat the other part (the weaker and baser part). These two parts were thought of as forces 'straining towards different goals and working against one another like the two horses of a team' (1986a:67). But, Foucault warns, we should not therefore think of the 'inferior' part as being *outside* the self or as alien to it. The self, as a whole, *was* the team. Hence the exercise (or *askesis*) was not simply combative; it was also 'to cross swords with oneself' (1986a:68).

The goal of self-mastery was, therefore, victory over oneself: either a complete elimination of all desires or, more usually, the establishment of a permanent state of moderation, impervious to the 'violence' of those desires. Foucault points out that Socrates' famous act of self-testing—in which he lay with his beloved Alcibiades but did not give in to his sexual urges—did not eliminate all of Socrates' desires. They remained, but under much better control, never getting the worse of him. This is quite different from those Christian forms of self-examination and purification which are designed to *expunge* all 'immoralities'. Indeed, Aristotle held that the victory which *retains* the newly controlled desires is greater than that by which they are totally eliminated. It displays a greater state of virtue. Virtue, therefore, 'was not conceived as a state of integrity, but as a relationship of domination' (1986a:70). Foucault calls this the 'heautocratic' aspect of ethics: government of and by the soul.

This type of self-mastery had its corollaries in domestic and civic life. To rule one's desires was equivalent to ruling one's servants and one's spouse; thus lack of self-control was in parallel with bad housekeeping. And desires can be compared to the low-ranking population of the city-state which the wise ruler will dominate, although not by tyranny and the raw exercise of violent authority, for such behaviour would again show a lack of mastery of oneself. Like desires, the lower classes were accepted as having a legitimate existence: but either to oppress them or allow them to run free would betoken self-indulgence in the ruler.

The mastery of one's soul did not simply just happen. Instead it relied on that central aspect of the Greek arts of existence: *askesis*, training or exercise. It was not sufficient to be aware of ethical principles ('in theory'); they had to be practised, trained for in an almost gymnastic fashion, materially. And since self-mastery was related to civic mastery, this soul-training was often linked to the educational (and pederastic) role of the philosopher in advising those young noblemen who would one day rule the city. The theme of this ascetics, then, was the *epimeleia heautou*, the 'care of the self' (1986a:73) which was to become so important in the later pre-Christian era that Foucault takes it for the title of the third volume of his *History of Sexuality*. But for the ancient Greeks, it involved a co-operation in the training of body and mind in tandem, and this is connected with the 'strategy of need': the body must practise suffering and privation so that it can cope with them when they actually arise in order to be able to continually meet 'nature's minimum' under all circumstances and regardless of provision. In the midst of great pleasure (or a cornucopia of food and drink), or when one is deprived of the object of pleasure (or of wine or bread), the same minimum need must be met. Training (*askesis*)—undergoing the conditions of glut and scarcity—was the only thing to ensure this. In this respect, the 'rehearsal' for and the actual 'performance' of virtue were identical substances.

Yet, by the first and second centuries AD, the aspect of preparation and training (the care of the self) had become something to be pursued for its own sake. By this later stage, civic and domestic ascetics (training for the government of others) had become separate from ethical ascetics (training for the government of the self). This is the major shift in emphasis between the two periods described in Foucault's second and third volumes. But before we can trace his thinking on this shift, we must deal with the final aspect of ancient Greek ethics: its outcome, goal, or mode of fulfilment.

This 'teleological' aspect of the ethics is captured by the term *sophrosyne*, moderation: a state of being which brings the practitioner (the 'artist' of existence) to freedom. Nowadays it seems paradoxical that freedom should arise from self-restraint. But ancient Greek ethics was quite different on this score. To begin with, the parallel between the self and the city meant that not only must the city be free from conquest by its neighbouring states but each citizen must also be free from the enemies within. Unless both conditions pertained, true freedom could not arise. This freedom, therefore, was not the same as the existentialist concept of the 'free will': for its 'polar opposite was not a natural determinism, nor was it the will of an all-powerful agency: it was enslavement' (1986a:79). To give in to one's desires, to lack self-restraint, was to become a slave to, rather than a master of, *oneself*.

But this is the negative aspect of that freedom. Its positive aspect was that it was a form of power in its own right, 'a power that one brought to bear on oneself in the power that one exercised over others' (1986a:80). The control of sexual passion was linked indelibly to civic government: a single form of power. The good ruler was master of his passions, his 'self-rule moderated his rule over others' (1986a:81). In this respect, the perennial question of who should rule the ruler was answered by the natural condition of the good ruler: that he is in fact the ruled. He ruled himself before he ruled others. This guaranteed a single freedom which was (incidentally) both ethical and civil.

A major theme in the ethical goal of mastery was the related concept of virility. Men ruled cities and households: therefore the ruling part of the self ought to be its most manly part. This meant that there was a domain of specifically *ethical* virility which, as it came to dominance, ensured one's full existence as a free man. It was 'this prior condition of "ethical virility" that provided one with the right sense of proportion for the exercise of "sexual virility," according to a model of "social virility"' (1986a:83). Significantly, this did not mean that women ought to be ruled, in turn, by their most *feminine* natures. On the contrary, women were held capable of being 'masters' of themselves, of training *their* most virile part to rule their own self-relations. This meant—again paradoxically for modern societies—the existence of two positive characteristics in virile women: 'strength of character and dependence on the man' (1986a:84). In effect, women of virtue had to overcome their femininity in so far as this was associated with passivity, for 'immoderation derives from a passivity that relates it to femininity' (1986a:84). And, according to this same principle, a man who gave in to his feminine side, to passivity, displayed his weakness, his unfitness to rule either himself or others. Foucault notes, at this stage, that such passive men were not associated necessarily with pederasty. In Greece it was possible for a man to display his passivity/femininity in his relations with *women* via immoderation: too frequent intercourse, intercourse at the wrong time, and so on. Again, for us today, this is an odd arrangement: 'No one would be tempted to label as effeminate a man whose love for women leads to immoderation on his part' (1986a:85). On the contrary, this is almost *the* mark of today's 'masculine character'. The similar-looking embargoes on 'effeminacy' in the ancient and modern eras could not, in fact, be more different as soon as one looks at the broader ethical and conceptual fields which give them their meaning.

Freedom, then, is the natural corollary of self-restraint. But truth itself is the corollary of freedom. How does this arise? How are *sophrosyne* and truth ultimately linked? This has to do with the concept of the *logos*, that form of natural reason by which one arrives at the truth. For to rein in one's desires is to bring them under the control of this form of reason. In developing one's capacity for self-control, one simultaneously develops the capacity for reason which is the implement of that control. And in developing reason, one comes closer to truth. The moderate man will desire only 'what the rational principle directs' (1986a:86). Three further principles connected truth with proper sexual conduct. A structural principle placed the *logos* 'in a position of supremacy' (1986a:86): a basic assumption was that the 'reasonable part' of a man is most fitting to rule (1986a:87). An instrumental principle made reason the most useful or practical part of the self—this was what guaranteed that form of modesty which knew how to adapt to 'needs, times, and circumstances' (1986a:87). An ontological principle required a basic condition for both truth and self-mastery to emerge—namely, a knowledge of the self by the self.

Foucault argues that this ancient association between mastery, freedom and truth is ultimately very different from our modern idea that one's 'true sex' is to be extracted from within by, for example, confession or psychiatric examination. These modern techniques he calls 'the decipherment of the self' or the 'hermeneutics of desire' (1986a:89). But in the Platonic tradition it constituted an 'aesthetics of existence' (1986a:89, 1989:309–16), comprising a set of general (if formal) principles rather than a strict moral code. It orients itself not towards the truth of the self as a goal in itself but towards a practical way of life.

Foucault closes his discussion of the aesthetics of existence (*as* a relation to truth) by quoting a number of passages from Xenophon, Plato and Aristotle. Together they attest to the idea of a proper 'order of things'. But this 'structuration' of the cosmos never stands alone. It is brought back to the problem of order (or disorder) in the soul. This in turn is connected to the question of which part of the soul must rule which. The response is always couched in terms of reason and temperance. And the instance of this temperance is always 'the right kind of love' (1986a:90). To love properly, then, is not simply to be a good citizen, but also to make one's life a work of art—to be a noble resident of the true cosmic order. This has absolutely nothing to do with legal-moral codes which carefully specify which acts are permitted or outlawed. How is the long journey between these two utterly different forms of regulating self, sex and truth accomplished? Foucault took it to its next stage: up to 200 AD.

Sex and the self from Plato to Plutarch

The third volume of *The History of Sexuality* (1988) traces the differences between pagan sexual ethics in and around the fourth century BC and the sexual ethics of imperial Rome and Greece in the first two centuries of our era. A number of general changes are immediately noticeable (1988:67ff). First, there is a new emphasis away from *chresis* (use) and towards *epimeleia*, 'the concern for oneself'. This slightly more recent concept means to have a concern for one's self or one's soul and also to get involved with something ('to bother with'). It is not simply a spiritual but also a material practice: *epimeleia* hardly distinguishes between soul and body. Secondly, this is a much more social (and uniformly social) art than the ascetics of Plato and Xenophon. That is, it stresses the arts of living as practices which have as much to do with a man's concern for others (especially his wife) as with himself. Thirdly, while the theme of struggle for self-domination is still apparent in the period up to 200 AD, it acquires a new emphasis on the *weakness* of the individual and his need to find shelter and protection (in the household and the family particularly). Fourthly, the new arts of the self are much less socially discriminating: they are written in such a way as to be directed to everyone; they refer 'to universal principles of nature and reason' (1988:67). But for all this, the ethical principles do not become anything like a legislated moral code. They are simply more widespread and less given to fine distinctions between what is proper for whom, when and where. Fifthly, the forms of training or exercise (*askesis*) are given over much more directly to self-knowledge. Their main maxim appears to be: go directly as possible to the truth of oneself. Lastly, while domination is still a goal in its own right it has added to it a new aspect of *enjoyment*, of pleasing oneself 'without desire and without disturbance' (1988:68). In summary, while many themes remain, they are modified—in some cases cut short, in others extended into new fields—to produce 'a new stylistics of existence' (1988:71). These general transformations have particular effects in the three main fields common to the two eras: the body (medicine), the household (economics) and the question of the love of boys (erotics): life, labour and love. We must now look at each of these in more detail.

The ancient art of medicine was very unlike our own. It placed little emphasis on pathology, correction and cure. In matters of sexuality, its 'problematization of sexual behavior was accomplished less out of a concern for eliminating pathological forms than out of a desire to integrate it as fully as possible into the management of health and the life of the body' (1986a:98). Accordingly, its main process involved *diate* (regimen), which covered the field of health in general and integrated sexual health with questions of exercise, sleep, food and drink. This general field of medicine remained largely unchanged during the immediate pre-Christian era. In a number of particular alterations, however, new stresses and tensions begin to emerge.

The medicine of the 'imperial' era was formed as a *logos* (a reasoning) about and for everyday life and its functioning. At the same time, it was far from being the 'profession' we have today. Rather, it was expected that the arts of medicine would be practised by everyone; everybody was to be their own health counsellor (1988:101). As with the ancient 'doctors', the medical thinkers at the turn of the millennium related questions of illness and health to place and time. Certain rooms of the house were thought to have their own health benefits. Different times of the year required different dietary and exercise habits. So while the ancient concern with 'the right time' and 'the right place' continued to thrive in the later period, there was also a 'tighter structuring of life . . . a more constantly vigilant attention to the body' (1988:103). As with many of the other principles we will encounter from this time, there is a distinct feeling that regimes were becoming firmer; that they were *moving towards* a moral code without actually attaining it.

With regard to sexuality, there was now a greater emphasis on its function as nature's proper path to eternity. The belief was—and this too can be found in the thought of the earlier period—that nature had contrived sexual reproduction as a mechanism by which humanity could continue while its individual members died. Death, of course, was a natural occurrence; but nature was also on the side of life. Sexual reproduction solved this contradiction, offering a 'bridge' from the death of the individual to the continuation of 'the species'. Sex provided nature's solution to her own problem (1988:105). Accordingly, sexuality became 'naturalised' through association with bodily excretions. Placed among the excretions, sex could be linked to the organism as a whole and also made into 'a process in which the individual's health, and possibly his very life, is at risk' (1988:107). So, by contrast with ancient thinking, the sexual medicine of Galen and Hippocrates tended to construct desire and pleasure much more organically. It placed them on the side of the body.

One outcome of this was an increase in what might be called 'spermocentrism', a high valuation of the seminal secretion. It was now linked closely to the breath and to vitality. In antiquity, it is true, the philosophers had thought of sperm as a coagulation of the other bodily fluids, building up and finally being ejaculated—but the process was thought necessary only in order to pass the essence of the father on to his offspring. But Galen associated the coagulated fluid with the *pneuma*, the essential breath or life-force which discharged it (1988:108). Hence the disease associated with effeminacy (gonorrhea, over-ejaculation) came to be explained in terms of a loss of vitality. A further consequence of making the question of sex—via ejaculation—more bodily (and, perhaps, less ethical) was to associate it with other kinds of bodily tremors and convulsions, especially epileptic fits. The final moment of the sexual act, therefore, had now come to be thought of as a spasm: as with epilepsy (which was believed to be the expulsion of an excess of cerebral humour), its primary agent was the body. Its mechanisms, its relations of fluids, nerves and muscles, were central to an understanding of one's sexuality. This nexus of nature, body and disease was not unknown to Platonic medicine; but it is a far cry from that earlier, almost purely dietetic, knowledge of sex.

On the question of whether sexual pleasure was 'good' or 'bad', medical thought in the period to 200 AD had much more definite ideas. The ancient Greeks, let us remember, tended to assign positive or negative ethical value to sexual conduct mostly in terms of its proper timing and the particular statuses of the participants. In the new era, there arose the question of whether having sex *at all* was good or bad. And because sex was now considered more in terms of its corporeal aspects (ejaculation in particular), a new ambivalence arose. Sex acts and (or as) the *production* of sperm were good, for they were on the side of life, health and vitality. But the *expenditure* of sperm, at the same time, was a vital loss and therefore bad (1988:112–13). In the space of this ambivalence, the sexual act became fragile and precarious, especially in terms of its continual linkage to non-sexual diseases (1988:116). Therefore having sex could be a therapy; there were particular diseases for which it was thought a beneficial tonic. Hippocrates argued that 'sexual intercourse is excellent against diseases due to the phlegm' (1988:118). But at the same time it could be a cause of illnesses. 'It makes weak people warm again', said Galen, 'but afterwards it chills them considerably' (1988:119). The point of the newly emergent sexual medicine was the calculation of circumstances. The ancient and almost purely ethical question of 'when to have sex' came to be answered (perhaps even 'diagnosed') in terms of its location on a loose table of diseases and their cures.

In all of this—and for quite different reasons from those of the ancient dietary regimen—abstention was thought, on the whole, to be beneficial. Ditto virginity (1988:121). Needless to say, this valorisation of continence was quite different again from that of the later Christian period. It was less a matter of holiness and purification—though it did have its part to play in the preparation for marriage—than of prevention and cure. The medical counsel of Galen, Hippocrates and Soranus, like that of the ancient Greeks, still lacked a precise typology of sexual acts. Instead, a loose set of maxims on forms of intercourse informed a general knowledge about types of progeny: different practices would produce relatively good or bad offspring (1988:125). Hence there were effectively prohibitions on (or at least advice against) intercourse during menstruation, after drinking and during pregnancy. These prohibitions are familiar enough today. But again, if both Soranic medicine and Christian morality advise against sex during menstruation, this is where the similarity stops. If, for Christianity, it is a defilement associated with uncleanliness and unholiness, then for Soranus, it was more or less a waste of sperm—the menstrual blood might sweep it out (1988:126).

Pagan dietetics, it is true, had its regimen of proper ages for the *aphrodisia*, but the new calculation was based much more on the possible effects that age in combination with sexuality might have on health. For example, puberty was taken as an obvious, organically based, guideline for the calculation of the proper age. However, the boy's ability to ejaculate was, in itself, not sufficient for him to be thought ready for sexual activity. Rather 'several years should pass during which the body is forming the seminal liquids without it being advisable to evacuate them' (1988:129). With girls, though with exceptions, there was less emphasis on waiting. Once her menstrual periods were occurring regularly, it was thought the girl was fit for marriage and childbearing. So the calculation of age now came to be based on questions of bodily maturity. The same medicalisation is evident in the question of the proper time for sexual intercourse. Its seasonability was a quite different matter from the ancient Greek concept of timeliness, since it had less to do with 'the proper amount' than with digestion (in its turn associated with the ingestion and secretion of fluids). 'That is why coitus in the middle of the night is deceptive, because then the food is not yet elaborated; the same is true of coitus that one has early in the morning, because there still may be ill-digested food in the stomach and because all the superfluities have not yet been evacuated through the urine and feces' (1988:131). In addition to this, certain personal temperaments and activities were thought more or less conducive to sexual activity. Horseback riding, for example, was thought good, while javelin-throwing was too violent (1988:132).

Sexuality had clearly become a much more bodily matter. But this did not mean that the soul had no part to play. It, too, had to be trained—but only because it was thought that mental control was the best way of staying on the 'track' of the organism's necessities (1988:133). Crucial to this was a new harmonisation of the body's desires with those of the soul. But what this synchrony sought to avoid was the body being *led* by the soul, particularly by its faculty of imagination (1988:135). In particular, the new physicians distrusted certain mental images. The practice of sex had to be set up so as to be led by the organism's functioning rather than by these images of desire. And at the same time, sexual relations had to be organised so as not to *induce* such images. Hence it was thought favourable to have sex modestly, in the dark, when the sight of the lover's body would not produce its own excitement. But curiously enough, this advice on the misuse of images was not established as a prohibition on masturbation—though it may sound very like the nineteenth-century view of 'sinful' images and their supposed production of seminal incontinence. On the contrary, the new physicians saw masturbation in a positive light, as 'an act of natural elimination, which has the value both of a philosophical lesson and a necessary remedy' (1988:140). In this new ensemble, then (which was by no means an 'economy'), the dictates of the organism were primary: chastity and continence consisted of relieving the body's urges rather than seeking the soul's pleasures (1988:139). And masturbation fitted this principle exactly. The idea of a sexual limit, insofar as it existed, was the limit of a certain calculation of the body's needs, with the soul committed almost exclusively to its service.

This slightly adjusted sexual ethics, however, paid—as with the Greeks—lesser attention to the sexual aspects of the overall art of living. As with them, the stress was much more on food and drink (1988:140). There was a new but very limited 'pathologisation' of the body generally and therefore of its sexuality. It was based on the problem of excess and the troubles peculiar to the very nature of sex, and produced correspondingly an increase in vigilance and a closer form of control. But this was far from being the kind of 'decipherment', the close and meticulous reading of each and every symptom, that later Christian doctrines required. What is interesting for us about this change in medicine, its conception of the body, and the position of the body within a sexual ethics, is its obvious continuities with the early Christian period and perhaps even with modern western societies. Such continuities, however, tend to deflect us from crucial differences. Foucault's lesson is clear: don't make history out of easy similarities; make it out of difficult differences.

The same is true in the sphere of the household, the *oikos* (from which our current term 'economics' arises). For the ancient Greeks, the household was important as a sexual sphere because it was part of the triple domain of self-control constituted by the self, the family and the city. By the time of Musonius' *Marriage Precepts* and Plutarch's *Dialogue on Love*, however, the household had assumed a quite different sexual function. During the first two centuries AD, a new intensification was accorded to conjugality. A man's wife ceased to be simply one of the 'objects' of his control and became, instead, what we might now call a 'significant other'. There was a correspondingly new stress on marriage as a tie between two relatively equal partners—each of whom was to be taken into account as an ethical subject. And more significantly, the marital tie itself became the central pivot of the self's social relations in general (1988:148).

If the Platonic regimen cast marriage primarily in terms of its civic and procreative functions, there was now a movement at a tangent, towards a new unity in marriage based on the idea of a primitive natural tendency. Marriage was reconstructed as a natural and, as it were, 'unified' binary or duality which allowed one's physical and social properties (one's nature and one's reason) to come together under a single rubric (1988:152–3). The old debate about whether it is 'better' or 'worse' to marry was transformed. Now marriage became a question of duty, and the debate centred on the precise obligations it carried. This duty, it was said, had been ordained by nature as a set of intrinsically *human* tasks and obligations (1988:155). There remained some contention, however, about whether philosophers should marry. Many thought they should not. But against this older view was set the argument that a philosopher ought to marry because marriage would make him a model of the proper life ordained by nature (1988:157).

So questions about the usefulness (or, indeed, uselessness) of marriage came to be replaced by a stress on *affect* in marriage. Marriage became the primary relation which was above blood relations: 'a whole mode of existence' (1988:159). As with the ancients, the household or *oikos* was still the locus of marriage, but there was now a new space 'behind' the sheer economic space of domestic organisation. It constituted a way of two persons living together as one person (1988:160). While the wife, in ancient Greece, was thought of as property, as a means of bearing legitimate descendants, Musonius and Plutarch spoke more directly in favour of the need for the *presence* of a man's wife as the main point from which his civic functions sprang and to which they should return. And, as a corollary, the presence of the husband equally anchored the wife's domestic function. Each was supposed to return to the other's presence as the source and outcome of their other (civic or domestic) lives (1988:160).

This established what Foucault refers to as a new kind of *dialogue*: an exchange of information, sympathy and encouragement for each partner's activities—effectively a kind of mutual affection (1988:161). One's wife became one's best friend. And while the earlier philosophers had taught that there ought to be distinct kinds of virtue for men and women, the thinkers around Plutarch spoke instead of 'an equal capability for virtue' (1988:161) which went by the name of *homonoia*. This new category required the marriage partners to be involved in a complete fusion. They were to become one person in two bodies and not simply a mixture which could easily be returned to its original components (1988:162).

Consequently the old dominion over oneself was not replaced. Rather, it was manifested in a new way, 'in the practice of obligations with regard to others', especially one's wife (1988:149). Hence marriage became the social space which had a *monopoly* on sexual relations. It was the only place where one could properly take one's sexual pleasures. The old relation between marriage and sex was centred on procreation, but by the second century AD, a conjugalisation of sex began to emerge. Sex became confined to marriage on the grounds that its very nature and origin was conjugal (1988:166). Marriage therefore became the natural home of sex, and this ethic was supported by the idea that extramarital sex might actually *hurt* the person of the wife and not simply (as before) because it would threaten her civic status (1988:167). Sex outside marriage, however, was rarely prohibited by direct precepts—at least as far as men were concerned. Rather, extramarital relations were thought to be bad for one's *self*. But what we can see emerging here is the *possibility* of legal precepts about marital fidelity—precepts which reconfigure the self as one who undertakes actions (or refrains from undertaking them) *for the sake of the other* (1988:168).

In the work of Musonius, however, there is an even stronger move towards a set of moral precepts. Here, for example, contraception is thought of as a transgression of the citizen's responsibility and his broader status as a natural (that is, rational social) being (1988:169). But again, it would be wrong to make a direct historical link between this injunction and a very similar one associated with Catholicism. For Musonius, contraception was not sinful, evil or against holy law. It was a waste, an immodest practice, an abuse of one's wife and a whole range of other negativities which showed the man who practised it to be a less than worthy citizen. Similarly, and on another front, adultery had once been considered a breach of civic trust between two men—the male adulterer, and the owner (father or husband) of his female lover. Reformulated in the new era, adultery came to be perceived as more a breach of *homonoia*, a couple's mutual respect, than of civic trust.

Foucault describes a 'strong' thesis about marriage which argues for an absolutely exact symmetry of relations-with-others for the wife and the husband. But he also marks the presence, at the time, of a weaker thesis which was much less preceptual in arguing for symmetrical fidelity as merely the proper and beneficial 'style'. According to the weak thesis, extramarital sex was actually a rather trivial matter—so unimportant, in fact, that a man should not threaten his wife by means of such a *minor* transgression. Extramarital sex became an issue which related to the husband's ethical weakness—it was not yet, quite, a legal tort.

What then of pleasure *within* the sphere of marriage? We can say, in regard to this, that the problems of pleasure in marriage at least came to greater prominence than ever before in being opened up for a much fuller scrutiny (1988:149). This tended to replace the ancient questions about marriage in terms of its role in the life of the city. But at the same time, this new problematisation was accompanied by a considerable reserve on the part of the philosophers when it came to specifying and valuing particular sexual *acts* (1988:176). Musonius, for example, located sexual pleasure as only *one* of the three marital 'deities': Hera, Eros *and*

Aphrodite. This meant that there was a new injunction not to treat one's spouse as purely a lover—a creature of Aphrodite—for this would reduce the spouse's sense of selfhood (1988:177). Marriage, that is, remained the site of two ancient *purposes*: the production of descendants and the creation of a space of 'shared life'. To reconstruct it as purely a site of pleasure would work contrary to these main functions (1988:177–8). Thus, while marriage was the only lawful place for pleasure, that pleasure had to be conducted austerely and with proper respect (1988:178).

The first purpose of marriage (procreation), at this time, led only to the most general recommendations about the sexual act: it should not take place during menstruation or pregnancy. These injunctions, however, were matters of ethical principle and not elements of a code (1988:179). The second purpose (provision of a shared life) also called for certain austerity measures. The wife had become a companion: to have sexual relations with her too frequently would therefore be an assault to her dignity (again, not simply to her civic status). These two purposes meant that marriage became a 'rapprochement' between men and women, and it was thought at the time that proper sexual pleasures could not help but cement that rapprochement. Hence sexual pleasure was naturally good (1988:180). It then became necessary to solve philosophically the paradoxical mismatch between 'necessary austerity and desirable intensity' (1988:180). Its solution lay in the idea that marital fidelity and modesty (being faithful, confining sex to the darkness, and so on) could actually be forms of sexual attraction (1988:180). Effectively, spouses were expected to be impassioned by each other's faithfulness and sexual reserve.

As Foucault (1988:182–5) notes, these new stresses—on the 'art of conjugal relationship', on a 'doctrine of sexual monopoly', and on 'an aesthetics of shared pleasures' (1988:149)—were quite distinct from the marital ethics of the earlier period. At the same time, they were just as distant from the marital *codes* of the Christian period.

But it was perhaps in the sphere of 'the love of boys' that the changes in ethics were felt most obviously. Overall, it was subject to a much less intense scrutiny, and for several reasons: the relative unimportance of pederasty for the Romans, who also exacted much tighter controls—by fathers over sons; changes in the organisation of the educational system, with teachers being expected to act *in loco parentis* and therefore to exercise greater vigilance over their young charges; and a greater valorisation of marriage as the proper space of sexuality (1988:189).

Pederasty in Platonic times had been debated via the comparative merits of the two possible types of love for boys: 'eros' or pure love and 'aphrodite' or physical love. This duality came to be replaced by another debate: the comparison between love of boys and love of women (1988:191). Foucault describes this as a new 'crossroads' (1988:195). The form of the debate is similar, but the two possible 'paths' of choice were radically altered. Hence another paradox: 'it is around the question of pleasure that reflection on pederasty developed in Greek antiquity; it is around this same question that it will go into decline' (1988:192).

Eros (pure love), which was once reserved exclusively for boys, came to be a feature of the marital relation—and almost completely restricted to that relation. In Plutarch's dialogue, the variables are newly delimited in exactly this way. He begins with what we would now call a 'moral tale' in which a *woman* comes to take on all the features of the *erastes* (the lover of a boy). Hence the old choice between physical and pure love is transformed: it becomes a choice between the pure love of women (including pleasure) and the immodest love between men. The values once associated with pederasty are transferred to conjugal love (1988:197).

In the old regime, where there was a single form of the *aphrodisia* and a double erotics (pure/physical), the question of the 'object' (male/female) did not figure so prominently. In the new regime there was instead a unitary form of love and a stricter boundary between its application to boys and to women (1988:198). Proper erotics moved, that is, into the field of relations between men and women, making a single domain of love. This transferral then effectively disqualifies male–male sexual relations as improper (1988:199).

Some arguments *against* love for women survived from the earlier philosophies, especially the argument that because intercourse with a woman is natural it is animalistic and therefore not proper for rational beings, who should overcome the mere urges of nature towards rutting and breeding (1988:200). On this argument, the love for women would always contain the baser element of pleasure, while the purer love for boys would always be detached from it (at least potentially) and tend towards nobility. But Plutarch denounces these philosophers of pederasty as hypocrites: they speak of purity, he argues, but are really only interested in the physical side of sex with boys (1988:201). Against them, he argues that Eros comes into the sphere of love for women by virtue of being a true god and not merely an abstract passion. In this way Plutarch is able to appropriate the themes of the old erotics and relocate them in the new field that we would recognise today as 'heterosexual' (1988:202).

Plutarch begins with an argument about the purity of love as such before considering its application in the two possible domains: women *or* boys (1988:203). He goes on, however, to say that only the first domain involves true friendship, via the complete fusion of the man and his wife into a single being (1988:204). Eros is akin, therefore, to the modesty of the conjugal relation itself. By comparison with such a monument to pure love, pederasty is bound to be imperfect (1988:205). Plutarch then confronts the classical dilemma over pederasty: it will either be a matter of conquest and violence (by the man over the boy), or else involve unvirile passivity. But he takes this argument to a new conclusion, namely that pederasty is therefore 'ungraceful' (*acharistos*) (1988:206). This was a conclusion unknown to the philosophers of antiquity, for whom the dilemma merely marked a category of problem for philosophical and ethical debate.

By contrast with pederasty, marriage, through its natural grace (*charis*), was supposed to lead to true and pure friendship (1988:206). Pleasure, then, was central to marriage. Pleasure could be seen as actually *founding* marriage: but, in turn, marriage was the only space where pleasure could be kept within the bounds of propriety (1988:208). Nevertheless, Plutarch's position was by no means the only one available. The pro-pederastic tradition did not simply disappear because of the new comparisons between it and marriage. *Affairs of the Heart* (attributed to Lucian), indeed, rehearses all of the old themes of 'which love?' and returns a verdict in favour of pederasty (1988:211–27).

Yet for Foucault, the contrast between these two advocates of the different types of love (Plutarch and Lucian) is not founded on differences between two moral codes. Nor is it a question of absolute moral (still less legal) prescriptions. Rather, it is a contrast of 'two forms of life' (1988:218). It is a lighthearted debate between these two styles, and one which—despite the virtues of marriage—openly countenances the virtues of pederasty as a practice which does not have to be excluded simply because one is married (1988:226).

For us today, approaching the end of another millennium, this is an almost unthinkable debate about sexual ethics. All of its variables have altered inextricably. Or to quote a much earlier Foucault: 'In the wonderment of this . . . the thing we apprehend in one great leap, the thing that, by means of the fable, is demonstrated as the exotic charm of another system of thought, is the limitation of our own, the stark impossibility of thinking *that*' (1970:xv). Now although the first volume of *The History of Sexuality* (1979a) dealt to some extent with modern ethical questions, it did so almost exclusively in terms of its earliest moral codes, its decipherments and its taxonomies of permitted acts and perversions. And the planned fourth volume (*The Confessions of the Flesh*) was presumably going to move the history of ancient sexual ethics into what Foucault calls the Christian period. But the question remains: what of the subject and sexual ethics today? The volumes we have been describing in this chapter make constant allusions to differences between ancient, imperial, Christian and modern ethics. But they remain allusive. Is it possible to imagine how Foucault's ideas might be 'applied' to the contemporary ethical scene, fraught as it is today with new questions of the relations between sexuality and, especially, gender? Foucault obviously thought so:

> From Antiquity to Christianity, we pass from a morality that was essentially the search for a personal ethics to a morality of obedience to a system of rules. And if I was interested in Antiquity it was because, for a whole series of reasons, the idea of a morality as obedience to a code of rules *is now disappearing, has already disappeared.* And to this absence of morality corresponds, must correspond, the search for an aesthetics of existence (1990:49 our italics).

Gender and sexuality: continuing problems

It is quite wrong to think of Foucault's last works as involving simply a 'return of the subject' or a shift 'from the body to the self' (McNay, 1992:48). These works certainly manifest a new *tension* in Foucault's continuing concern with the subject: it is overtly ethical in a quite new way. But this has more to do with the historical specificity of the ancient societies he was investigating than with a radical theoretical shift. Still less, as McNay *does* point out, is it a 'retraction' (Ferry and Renaut, 1990) or complete rethinking of 'his previous work, which so systematically attacked and undermined the notion of the subject' (McNay, 1992:48; O'Farrell, 1989). On the contrary, Foucault *at no point* 'attacked and undermined' the idea of a subject which has knowledge of (and a relation to) itself. It was simply that such a version of the subject was not pertinent to studies of the historical emergence of modern forms of incarceration and the legal, scientific and religious 'policing' of sexual practice. The field of ethics (as the relation of the self to itself) has been, perhaps sadly, a relatively minor concern in what might be called the modern sexual field. And it is by virtue of his continuing insistence on showing how things could now be (and could have been) otherwise that Foucault turned, in his last works, to that particular 'otherwise' constituted by ancient societies which did indeed ground their ideas of correct sexual comportment in the self itself, in the ethical, in the subject as different from (and other than) a mere external body. To say this is not to neglect or de-emphasise the critical importance in Greece and Rome of the cultivation of the body as one of the main objects on which these ancient ethics acted, and perhaps to an even *greater* degree than modern techniques have done.

Mistaking Foucault's problematic—by discerning a radical shift *towards* the self in his last works—can lead to peculiar conclusions. McNay, for example, concludes quite wrongly that 'Foucault appears to be relatively uninterested in exploring the intersection of sexuality with an understanding of the self' (1992:193). She can say this only because she fails to grasp the radically different way in which Foucault uses the term 'sexuality'—that is, in a way quite distinct from any notion of *essentially* gendered subjects. A related but different problem arises with Diprose (1987, 1991), who discounts any mention of Foucault's historical construction of sexuality. Her analysis of Foucault on the question of sexual difference omits a discussion of *his* conception of sexuality. While Diprose claims not to be dismissing the value of Foucault's approach to ethics, her neglect of the issue of sexuality acts as a dismissal, for it reveals a superficial understanding of the connections between his ethical work and the earlier concerns with discourse and power. She attributes to Foucault's studies of normalising techniques (1977a, 1979a) a concern with 'embodiment', namely the effects that power produces on the body.

But by far the most significant feature of Foucault's thesis on power and its relationship to the body is its connection with the historical emergence of 'sexuality' in conjunction with these techniques. Moreover, Foucault explicitly places his later ethical work within this problematic. He states that his intention is to 'dwell' on that 'quite recent and banal notion of sexuality' (1986a:3). Neither Greek nor Roman thought understood 'sexuality' as referring to 'a single entity' which allows 'diverse phenomena to be grouped together' (1986a:35). This was Foucault's reason for leaving Greek terms such as *aphrodisia* in their original form: they cannot be translated adequately into the terms we have come to use. His purpose was to overturn the conception that 'sexuality' is a human 'constant'. But in doing so, he discovered it was not enough to relate the emergence of sexuality to the formation of sciences and the systems of power peculiar to our epoch. He had to go further: he had to discover by what route human subjects had come to *subject themselves* to a 'hermeneutics of desire' (1986a:5). Importantly, all contemporary analyses of this self-subjection, whether traditional (sexology or biology) or critical (psycho-analysis), were 'dominated by the principle of "desiring man"' (1986a:5). Foucault thus sought to liberate analyses of sexual subjectivities from the tyranny of this ahistorical 'desiring man'.

Diprose overlooks this attempt by Foucault to differentiate our present regime of erotic practices from another. She therefore cannot register Foucault's insistence that our contemporary sexual subjectivities, and the 'ethics' derived from them, are based on scientistic conceptions of 'life' tied to recent devices of power. It is this which places his recommendations for an 'aesthetics of existence' into its correct context. It is not a recipe for idealistically making up bodies, as Diprose seems to suggest, but an intervention which sets itself in opposition to a 'science' of sexual practice. As Bernauer neatly puts it: 'To speak of human existence as a work of art is to take it out of the domain of the scientifically knowable and to free us from the obligation of deciphering ourselves as a system of timeless functions which are subjected to corresponding norms' (1988:129).

More seriously still, Diprose cannot help but reproduce precisely what Foucault was attacking: the tendency to equate 'sex' with 'sexuality', and thus miss the radical content of what he has to offer to feminism. Foucault sets these two concepts apart by explaining sexuality not in terms of 'sex', but in terms of a historical construct associated with modernity. While Diprose (1991:15) provides an account of sexual difference which *does not problematise* this conflation, Foucault's arguments open up the possibility that 'sexual difference' can be something other than the *sexualised* version of it we have inherited, and that the bodily differences between men and women can be conceived as something other than *sexual difference.* As Butler (1986:515) has noted, Foucault implicitly challenges those feminist positions which portray 'sexual difference as irreducible'.

An important aspect of Diprose's critique, however, is that Foucault's limited focus on *male* subjectivity fails to account for the construction of masculinity in relation to femininity. This may be a valid criticism. According to Diprose, Foucault does not acknowledge the 'debt to the other incurred in the constitution of one's ethos' (1991:13). Foucault conducts his investigations of sexual ethics by ignoring the inequality at the core of subjectivity, and failing to see that the production of a male body *depends on* the association of the female body with absence, chaos, fragmentation, undecidability, and so forth. Primarily, the constitution of identity cannot escape its relation to the other. But according to Diprose's understanding of the problem, all relations to the 'other' are constructed within a fundamental system of the generation of meaning. This system is dominated by an economy of the *logos*, a 'logocentric' economy where 'absence' is the precondition of 'presence'. If women's bodies become inscribed by the former term, then this means they are positioned as the 'conditions' of male subjectivity: 'the structure of the constitution of the self, whatever the technique, is that the self will be divided from itself, finding within its identity a trace of its other' (1991:13).

But Foucault fails to acknowledge this 'debt' for a very good reason: he does not subscribe to the notion that subjectivity can be reduced to the effects of an elementary relation. Indeed, reducing masculinity and femininity to the effects of the bodily differences between men and women is to analyse subjectivity exactly in the ways Foucault eschewed. For Foucault, there does not exist a *global* 'ethos' indebted to a *generalised* 'other'. It is quite contrary to those analyses of pluralistic struggles which characterise his work. In describing his own position as a public intellectual, Foucault claims: 'If I tell the truth about myself . . . it is in part that I am constituted as a subject across a number of power relations which are exerted over me and which I exert over others' (1990:39). The implication is that the 'number' of power relations operating simultaneously precludes singling out any particular one as the most fundamental.

Furthermore, when Foucault speaks of the 'other' in the context of explaining his later work, one way in which he does so is in a very specific *sexual* sense. A large part of Foucault's displacing of scientistic conceptions of sexuality is the attempt to conceive of erotic practices in terms of an ethics of pleasure. The male ethics Foucault describes could have special relevance to the *present* economy of bodies and pleasures. If a free man's relationship to his sexual 'other' in ancient Greek society in no way obliged reciprocity (and in fact quite the contrary), men in contemporary society must take account of this inequality. But by exposing the 'difference' of Greek practices in this area, Foucault shows that we have 'solved' the problem merely by democratising 'desire' in the process of democratising selfhood: that the 'other' must also be a subject who actively desires to be desired by another desiring subject. Foucault seems to be saying that this has not created circumstances which address the inequality inherent in sexual relations involving men, regardless of whether the man's 'other' is a woman *or* another man. We need to remember that his ethical work is read most fruitfully not as a 'theory' of selfhood but as a response to a problem of sexuality analysed historically:

> Are we able to have an ethics of acts and their pleasures which would be able to take into account the pleasure of the other? Is the pleasure of the other something which can be integrated in our pleasure, without reference either to law, to marriage, to I don't know what? (Foucault in Rabinow, 1987:346)

One could argue, therefore, that this dimension of sexuality is precisely what gets lost when one conceives of 'otherness', as Diprose does, in generalised terms of consciousness. It is much too convenient to think of the discourse of reciprocity as something concerning the mind and not 'acts and their pleasures'. While Diprose is certainly correct to highlight Foucault's lack of account of the effects of exclusion in the dominant public ethos of our society, her own solution is equally problematic. Just as power techniques and discourses cannot be attributed to a generalised *bourgeois* subject, neither can they be attributed to a general *male* subject. But Diprose's claim that alterity forms the conditions of male subjectivity fails to account for patriarchal power. It relies on a tautology: an inherent maleness must be assumed in the first place in order to account for that same identity. Essential masculinity is not located this time in psychological male subjects but in a primary textual process characterising western thought. But the effect is the same.

Diprose bases her argument on Derrida's (1976) analyses of how the constitution of presence characterises the history of western philosophy. But it is another thing again to transpose Derrida's insights into an all-encompassing and definitive account of the construction of ethical subjectivities. Diprose claims that Derrida 'locates a violence operating against the other—the effacement of the other involved in maintaining the assumption of autonomous self-present subjectivity' (1991:11). Yet it is not clear what creates this impulse to violence if it is also logically 'prior' to any subjects: an origin that is not an origin? But Diprose demands that it be associated with masculinity, for her whole point is to expose the greater male bias inherent in our logocentric system. This then requires an account of why the *male* body and not the female body is more inclined to inscribe itself with this greater tendency to mastery. As Rose points out (1986:21), 'identity' returns in these formulations as a 'psychic exigency' which seems to underpin the *logos.*

It is true that Foucault does not offer an account of the construction of sexual difference, nor of patriarchal power, although his work certainly challenges the *essentialist* notion of patriarchy. It shows that the ancient Greek attitude to wives involved treating women as mere property to be controlled. In imperial Rome, by contrast, the wife had status as an equal partner with the man. Woman as property, or woman as a variety of man: both are equally 'patriarchal' but totally different. And this begs the question of how a specifically modern (as opposed to an eternal and essential) patriarchy operates, in *its* specificity.

The critical relevance of Foucault's thesis on sexuality is that it offers a *materialist* ethics not derived from scientific knowledge. Moreover, Foucault's work provides the beginnings of an attempt to define *life* differently: life as 'aesthetics', but still a materialist conception of life. Immutable material facts—such as death and the different reproductive potentials of bodies—are not treated mystically or in accordance with a theology. But it differs from science in that existence can be modified by conscious artistry. One can attempt to 'transform' oneself in accordance with principles generated by shared aesthetic and moral standards. Foucault wants to remove 'art' from the domain of objective creativity and place it in the hands of a subject struggling to make itself a pleasurable and satisfying set of constructed experiences.

> What strikes me is the fact that in our society, art has become something which is related only to objects and not to individuals, or to life. That art is something which is specialised or which is done by experts who are artists. But couldn't everyone's life become a work of art? . . . From the idea that the self is not given to us, I think that there is only one practical consequence: we have to create ourselves as a work of art. (Foucault in Rabinow, 1987:350)

Foucault also offers the beginnings of the means to define *sexuality* differently. For him sexuality becomes primarily a set of acts conceived in non-scientistic and non-reproductive terms. As a tentative gesture, and in accordance with Foucault's ethics of pleasure, one could say that eroticism is a series of acts which must be conducted in terms of *reciprocity* of bodily pleasures. Importantly, this reciprocity is not 'given' but must be created. The notion of sexual reciprocity is a way of opposing both rape (that total lack of reciprocity) and the 'convenient' reference of this reciprocity to law or marriage arrangements. In a quite radical sense, then, Foucault's excursions into antiquity are very much part of his 'ontology of the present', and bear on the conditions under which we operate, and might *yet* operate, as sexual beings.

To read Foucault's work, then, as an 'ontology of the present' helps us understand why, during the last 'phase' of his work, tension shifts from the policing of bodies to an 'aesthetics of the self'. This stage of the work, as always, is a philosophy of 'otherwise', of transformations in one's *own* thinking which, for Foucault at least, can be the only reason for doing philosophy in the first place. His account of philosophical practice, we hope, is also an account of our own continuing 'essay' on Foucault:

> What is philosophy today—philosophical activity, I mean—if it is not the critical work that thought brings to bear on itself? In what does it consist, if not in the endeavor to know how and to what extent it might be possible to think differently, instead of legitimating what is already known? There is always something ludicrous in philosophical discourse when it tries, from the outside, to dictate to others, to tell them where their truth is and how to find it, or when it works up a case against them in the language of naive positivity. But it is entitled to explore what might be changed, in its own thought, through the practice of a knowledge that is foreign to it. The 'essay'—which should be understood as the assay or test by which, in the game of truth, one undergoes changes, and not as the simplistic appropriation of others for the purpose of communication—is the living substance of philosophy, at least if we assume that philosophy is still what it was in times past . . . an 'ascesis,' *askesis*, an exercise of oneself in the activity of thought. (1986a:8–9)

Bibliography

Althusser, L. (1976) *Essays in Self-Criticism*, London: New Left Books [Fr 1973–75]

Althusser, L. with E. Balibar (1970) *Reading Capital*, London: New Left Books [Fr 1968]

Anderson, R. and W. Sharrock (1986) *The Ethnomethodologists*, London: Tavistock

Austin, J. L. (1975) *How to do Things with Words*, Oxford: Oxford University Press

Barthes, R. (1967) *Elements of Semiology*, London: Cape [Fr 1964]

—— (1972) 'Authors and Writers' in *Critical Essays*, Evanston, Illinois: Northwestern University Press [Fr 1964]

—— (1977) 'The Death of the Author' in *Image-Music-Text*, Glasgow: Fontana/Collins [Fr 1968]

—— (1978) *A Lover's Discourse: Fragments*, New York: Hill & Wang [Fr 1977]

—— (1981) *Camera Lucida: Reflections on Photography*, New York: Hill & Wang [Fr 1980]

Bartky, S. (1988) 'Foucault, Femininity, and the Modernization of Patriarchal Power' in Diamond and Quinby (eds) *Feminism and Foucault*, pp. 61–86

Bauman, R. and J. Sherzer (eds) (1974) *Explorations in the Ethnography of Speaking*, Cambridge: Cambridge University Press

Bennett, T. (1992) 'Useful Culture' *Cultural Studies* 6, 3, pp. 395–408

Benterrak, K., S. Muecke and P. Roe (1984) *Reading the Country: Introduction to Nomadology*, Fremantle, WA: Fremantle Arts Centre Press

Bernauer, J. (1988) 'Beyond Life and Death: On Foucault's Post-Auschwitz Ethic' *Philosophy Today* 32, 2, pp. 128–42

Braidotti, R. (1991) *Patterns of Dissonance*, Cambridge: Polity Press

Burchell, G., C. Gordon and P. Miller (eds) (1991) *The Foucault Effect: Studies in Governmentality*, London: Harvester

Butler, J. (1986) 'Variations on Sex and Gender: Beauvoir, Wittig and Foucault' *Praxis International* 5, 4, pp. 505–16

Canguilhem, G. (1968) *Études d'histoire et de philosophie des sciences*, Paris: Vrin

Coulter, J. (1979) *The Social Construction of Mind*, London: Macmillan

Coward, R. and J. Ellis (1977) *Language and Materialism: Developments in Semiology and the Theory of the Subject*, London: Routledge & Kegan Paul

Culler, J. (1975) *Structuralist Poetics: Structuralism, Linguistics and the Study of Literature*, London: Routledge & Kegan Paul

Derrida, J. (1976) *Of Grammatology*, Baltimore: The Johns Hopkins University Press

Diamond, I. and L. Quinby (eds) (1988) *Feminism and Foucault: Reflections on Resistance*, Boston: Northeastern University Press

Diprose, R. (1987) 'The Use of Pleasure in the Constitution of the Body' *Australian Feminist Studies* 5, pp. 95–103

—— (1991) 'Foucault, Derrida and the Ethics of Sexual Difference' *Social Semiotics* 1, 2, pp. 1–21

Donzelot, J. (1980) *The Policing of Families*, London: Hutchinson

Dreyfus, H. L. and P. Rabinow (1982) *Michel Foucault: Beyond Structuralism and Hermeneutics*, Chicago: University of Chicago Press

Eco, U. (1986) *Travels in Hyper-Reality: Essays*, San Diego: Harcourt Brace Jovanovich

Eribon, D. (1992) *Michel Foucault*, London: Faber & Faber

Fairclough, N. (1989) *Language and Power*, London: Longman

Ferry, L. and A. Renaut (1990) *French Philosophy in the Sixties: An Essay on Antihumanism*, Amherst: University of Massachusetts Press

Forrester, J. (1990) *The Seductions of Psychoanalysis: Freud, Lacan and Derrida*, Cambridge: Cambridge University Press

Foucault, M. (1967) *Madness and Civilisation: A History of Insanity in the Age of Reason*, London: Tavistock [Fr 1961/1972]

—— (1970) *The Order of Things: An Archaeology of the Human Sciences*, London: Tavistock [Fr 1966]

—— (1971) 'Orders of Discourse: Inaugural Lecture Delivered at the Collège de France' *Social Science Information* 10, 2, pp. 7–30 [Fr 1971]

—— (1972) *The Archaeology of Knowledge*, London: Tavistock [Fr 1969]

—— (1973) *The Birth of the Clinic: An Archaeology of Medical Perception*, London: Tavistock [Fr 1963]

—— (1977a) *Discipline and Punish: The Birth of the Prison*, London: Allen Lane [Fr 1975]

—— (1977b) *Language, Counter-memory, Practice: Selected Essays and Interviews*, Oxford: Basil Blackwell

—— (1978a) *I, Pierre Rivière, having slaughtered my mother, my sister, and my brother . . . . A Case of Parricide in the 19th Century*, London: Peregrine [Fr 1973]

—— (1978b) 'Politics and the Study of Discourse' *Ideology and Consciousness* 3, pp. 7–26 [Fr 1968]

—— (1979a) *The History of Sexuality, Volume One: An Introduction*, London: Allen Lane [Fr 1976]

—— (1979b) 'Governmentality' *Ideology and Consciousness* 6, pp. 5–21

—— (1980a) *Power/Knowledge: Selected Interviews and Other Writings 1972–1977*, London: Harvester Press

—— (1980b) *Herculine Barbin*, London: Harvester Press

—— (1981) 'Questions of Method: An Interview with Michel Foucault' *Ideology and Consciousness* 8, pp. 3–14 [It 1978]

—— (1984) 'Le souci de la vérité: propos recueillis par François Ewald' *Magazine Littéraire* 207, pp. 18–23

—— (1986a) *The Use of Pleasure: The History of Sexuality Volume Two*, London: Viking [Fr 1984]

—— (1986b) 'Kant on Enlightenment and Revolution' *Economy and Society* 15, 1, pp. 88–96

—— (1988) *The Care of the Self: The History of Sexuality Volume Three*, London: Allen Lane/Penguin Press [Fr 1984]

—— (1989) *Foucault Live: Interviews, 1966–84*, New York: Semiotext(e) Foreign Agents Series

—— (1990) *Politics Philosophy Culture: Interviews and Other Writings 1977–1984*, New York: Routledge

Gadet, F. (1989) *Saussure and Contemporary Culture*, London: Hutchinson [Fr 1986]

Garfinkel, H. (1967) *Studies in Ethnomethodology*, Englewood Cliffs, New Jersey: Prentice-Hall

Giglioli, P. P. (ed.) (1982) *Language and Social Context*, Harmondsworth, UK: Penguin

Grace, W. (1992) Feminism Without Patriarchy?: Foucault's Dispersion of Total Histories, BA Hons, Murdoch University, Perth

Gumperz, J. D. and D. Hymes (eds) (1972) *Directions in Sociolinguistics: The Ethnography of Communication*, New York: Holt, Rinehart & Winston

Hacking, I. (1981) 'How Should We Do the History of Statistics?' *Ideology and Consciousness* 8, pp. 15–26

—— (1982) 'Bio-power and the Avalanche of Printed Numbers' *Humanities in Society* 5, pp. 279–95

Halliday, M. A. K. (1973) *Explorations in the Functions of Language*, London: Arnold

Harris, Z. S. (1952) 'Discourse Analysis' *Language* 28, pp. 1–30

Hawkes, T. (1977) *Structuralism and Semiotics*, London: Methuen

Hegel, G. W. F. (1977) *Phenomenology of Spirit*, Oxford: Clarendon Press [Ger 1807]

Heritage, J. (1984) *Garfinkel and Ethnomethodology*, Cambridge: Polity Press

Hesse, M. B. (1962) *Models and Analogies in Science*, London: Sheed & Ward

Hirst, P. and P. Woolley (1982) *Social Relations and Human Attributes*, London: Tavistock

Hodge, B. (1984) 'Historical Semantics and the Meanings of "Discourse"' *Australian Journal of Cultural Studies* 2, 2, pp. 124–3

Hodge, B. and G. Kress (1988) *Social Semiotics*, Cambridge: Polity Press

Kuhn, T. S. (1970) *The Structure of Scientific Revolutions*, Chicago: University of Chicago Press

Lane, M. (1970) 'Introduction' in *Structuralism: A Reader*, London: Cape, pp. 11–20

Lemon, L. and M. Reis (eds) (1965) *Russian Formalist Criticism: Four Essays*, Lincoln: University of Nebraska Press

Luke, C. (1989) *Pedagogy, Printing and Protestantism: The Discourse on Childhood*, Albany: State University of New York Press

Lydon, M. (1988) 'Feminism and Foucault: A Romance of Many Dimensions' in Diamond and Quinby (eds) *Feminism and Foucault*, pp. 135–48

McCarthy, M. (1992) 'Discourse Analysis' in T. McArthur (ed.) *The Oxford Companion to the English Language*, Oxford: Oxford University Press, pp. 316–17

Macdonell, D. (1986) *Theories of Discourse: An Introduction*, Oxford: Blackwell

McHoul, A. (1993) 'Discourse' in *The Encyclopedia of Language and Linguistics*, London: Pergamon

McNay, L. (1992) *Foucault and Feminism: Power, Gender and the Self*, Cambridge: Polity Press

Michaels, E. (1987) *For a Cultural Future: Francis Jupurrurla Makes TV at Yuendumu*, Melbourne: Artspace

Miller, J. (1993) *The Passion of Michel Foucault*, New York: Simon & Schuster

Miller, T. (1993) *The Well-Tempered Self*, Baltimore: The Johns Hopkins University Press

Mitchell, T. F. (1957) 'The Language of Buying and Selling in Cyrenaica' *Hesperis* 44, pp. 31–71

O'Farrell, C. (1989) *Foucault: Historian or Philosopher*, London: Macmillan

O'Regan, T. (1992) '(Mis)taking Policy: Notes on the Cultural Policy Debate' *Cultural Studies* 6, 3, pp. 409–23

O'Sullivan, T., J. Hartley, D. Saunders and J. Fiske (1983) *Key Concepts in Communication*, London: Methuen

Pêcheux, M. (1975) 'Analyse du discours, langue et idéologies' *Langages* 37, whole issue

Poster, M. (1984) *Foucault, Marxism and History: Mode of Production versus Mode of Information*, Cambridge: Polity Press

Rabinow, P. (ed.) (1987) *The Foucault Reader*, Harmondsworth, UK: Penguin

Rose, J. (1986) *Sexuality in the Field of Vision*, London: Verso

Sacks, H., E. A. Schegloff and G. Jefferson (1974) 'A Simplest Systematics for the Organization of Turn-taking for Conversation' *Language* 50, pp. 696–735

Sartre, J.-P. (1963) *Search for a Method*, New York: Vintage

—— (1982) *Critique of Dialectical Reason*, London: New Left Books

Saussure, F. de (1974) *Course in General Linguistics*, London: Fontana [Fr 1916]

Sawicki, J. (1986) 'Foucault and Feminism: Toward a Politics of Difference' *Hypatia* 1, 2, pp. 23–36

—— (1991) *Disciplining Foucault: Feminism, Power, and the Body*, New York: Routledge

Schegloff, E. A., G. Jefferson and H. Sacks (1977) 'The Preference for Self-correction in the Organization of Repair in Conversation' *Language* 53, pp. 361–82

Silverman, D. and B. Torode (1980) *The Material Word: Some Theories of Language and its Limits*, London: Routledge & Kegan Paul

Smart, B. (1983) *Foucault, Marxism and Critique*, London: Routledge & Kegan Paul

Spender, D. (1980) *Man-Made Language*, London: Routledge & Kegan Paul

Spivak, G. (1982) 'Displacement and the Discourse of Woman' in M. Krupnick (ed.) *Displacement: Derrida and After*, Bloomington: Indiana University Press, pp. 169–95

Tagg, J. (1988) *The Burden of Representation*, London: Macmillan

Threadgold, T. (1988) 'Language and Gender' *Australian Feminist Studies* 6, pp. 41–70

Turner, B. S. (1984) *The Body and Society: Explorations in Social Theory*, Oxford: Blackwell

Voloshinov, V. N. (1973) *Marxism and the Philosophy of Language*, New York: Seminar Press

Wickham, G. (ed.) (1987) *Social Theory and Legal Politics*, Sydney: Local Consumption Publications

Williams, R. (1973) 'Base and Superstructure in Marxist Cultural Theory' *New Left Review* 82, pp. 3–16

Williamson, D. (1989) *Authorship and Criticism*, Sydney: Local Consumption Publications

Index